Troubadour OF THE Troubled

The Meditations, Poems, and
Songs of Tam Duffill

COMPILED BY MARIANNE DUFFILL COX

Copyright 2015 Marianne Duffill Cox
All Rights Reserved
No part of this book may be reproduced, stored in a retrieval system, or transmitted by any means, electronic, mechanical, photocopying, recording, or otherwise without written permission from the author.

ISBN-13: 978-0692487013
ISBN-10: 0692487018

Introduction and Biography
Copyright 2015 Marianne Duffill Cox

Meditations, Poems, and Songs
Copyright 2015 Tamson Wailes Duffill

Photographs of Tam Duffill
Copyright 2015 Marianne Duffill Cox
and the Duffill Family *(except where attributed)*

Book Design & Formatting
Donna Overall
donnaoverall@bellsouth.net

Published by

LOIS COX PRESS

Marietta, GA

Table of Contents

Introduction 1

Biography 5

Tam Knew Talent 39

Some Old Friends Remember Tam 40

Meditations 43

Poems 113

Songs 169

Tam Is Still With Us 195

Words cannot express the thanks owed to Donna Overall for all her contributions to this book. She found the notebooks containing Tam's forty-five years of writing which were thought to be lost. We knew that they existed but didn't know where they were. She worked tirelessly to help me through the long process of completing this project. Her contacts with Tam's friends and fellow musicians from the '60s have made it possible for them to contribute to the book.

I would like to thank all those who contributed their stories and fond memories of Tam. I would like to thank Brian, Tam's brother, for allowing me access to the notebooks for the year and a half it has taken to complete this project. And finally I would like to thank my husband Chris Cox for his patience, understanding, and help with my lack of computer skills.

—Marianne Duffill Cox

Introduction

Tam and I were married for twenty years, and we knew each other for thirty-five years. We remained close even after we divorced. I knew him as well as anyone could know him. He was a very private person, as far as his feelings. Instead of talking to someone about his thoughts and feelings, he wrote about them. Writing was his emotional outlet and way of coping. Maybe he didn't completely trust people with his deepest feelings. Writing was a friend he could confide in and trust. The fifteen or so notebooks full of Tam's writings that were found after his death covered almost fifty years. I lived with Tam for nineteen years, and I never saw all these notebooks. He did show me a few of the poems when we were together, but not very many.

As you read the Meditations and Poems, you will notice that some words are misspelled. Tam was well educated, a college graduate, and very intelligent. Some misspelled words in the original writings, he marked "sp," meaning he knew they were misspelled and would have made the corrections later. Other times, he clearly meant to misspell the word, so I made the spelling corrections that were marked and not the ones that were obviously done on purpose.

In the section Tam calls "Meditations," I'm not sure if it would be called poetry or not, but the words flow poetically. They are wonderfully written snippets of time. He pays great attention to the details of simple, small moments observing nature and is able to put his thoughts down on paper so beautifully.

All Tam's writings are first drafts. He rarely went back to make any changes. "So Easy" *(See p. 47)* describes this style perfectly. In putting these writings together for this book, I have only added some punctuation and given some pieces titles.

The writings in the "Meditations" section were done in 1967 and 1968 while Tam was living in a cabin on a lake in north Georgia. It had electricity, but no heat or plumbing, and he had no TV, only a radio and, of course, his guitar and dog. The only income that he had at this time was singing and playing his guitar in nightclubs on weekends in Atlanta and sometimes in Athens.

Most of these writings were found on four by seven inch pieces of paper, held together by a rusty nail stuck through a hole in each page. No doubt he carried these pages with him as he went on his walks through the woods, around the lake, or in the city. He was able to keep these fragile papers for 45 years!

Also included in this section are some writings from the time that Tam worked at SCLC for Dr. Martin Luther King, Jr. He had quit teaching and was hired by Andrew Young to run the Varityper machine at SCLC in Atlanta. I think this was in 1966.

He was working at SCLC when Dr. King was killed and writes about his feelings during this time. He also describes scenes from the funeral. Tam was deeply affected by the deaths of both JFK, who was shot on Tam's birthday, November 22 of 1963, and the death of Dr. King on April 5, 1968. These were two of his heroes, and he felt it was a great injustice to lose such great men.

The last section features the lyrics of some of his songs. Unfortunately, we don't have the music to these lyrics because Tam never learned to read or write music. The tunes were in his head, as he played by ear. I tried to remember the tunes and pick them out on the piano, but had little luck. I decided to give up on that idea because my memory might be so far off that it would not do justice to Tam's work, so all we have are the lyrics.

Biography

It was a warm summer night in Atlanta on July 15, 1979. Having just moved from Athens to Atlanta, and not knowing anyone, I was happy to be invited to a party by my new roommate, Nancy. She had moved to Atlanta a year or so earlier from Athens. We had a lot of mutual friends back in Athens, and they had introduced us.

The party was in rural Doraville, a few miles north of Atlanta, in a big house where several guys lived. It was a scene right out of the '60s, even though it was 1979. Several guys were playing guitars, but one in particular stood out. He had long graying hair below his shoulders, a long full beard that was also graying, and his eyes were strikingly blue.

This was the night that I met Tam. During one of his breaks from playing, he came over and talked to me. The rest of the evening, he made lots of eye contact with me while he was playing and talked to me during each break.

By the end of the night, he was going home with me. Just as we were getting ready to leave, I went to say good night to my roommate. When I told her Tam was going home with me she said, "You know he tried to commit suicide by shooting himself in the head?" This shocking statement didn't faze me. My reply was, "I'm sure he'll tell me all about it." I was so smitten with Tam that it didn't put me off at all. He *did* go home with me that night, and he *did* tell me all about it.

And he never left. At first, we would go to his place every few days to get clothes or whatever else he needed. After a month or so, he moved in with me permanently and got rid of his place.

At the time, he had a Saint Bernard. He gave the dog to friends that lived in the country. That was all I asked him to do, because I had no yard to speak of, and it really wasn't fair to the dog to keep him in the city.

We settled into a routine. I was working at Crawford Long Hospital, and we were living on Fernwood Circle in Brookhaven in Atlanta. I took on the task of being his manager. I wrote up a resume and made a tape of him playing guitar and singing. I was able to get him several jobs in Little Five Points and in Buckhead. We married exactly one year later on July 15, 1980.

During this first year together, we took a road trip and drove to Colorado to visit some of his friends. Tam talked nonstop the entire trip. I even bet him that he couldn't be quiet for five minutes, and I won the bet.

He spent most of our spare time that first year telling me his life story. Most of these stories I remember well and will retell you in this biography. Tam's brother, Brian, has also contributed childhood stories and reaffirmed some of the ones I heard directly from Tam. I have also included some family history that Brian related to me and, of course, my time with Tam.

The eldest son of Olive and Monroe Duffill, Tamson Wailes Duffill was born in Bremerton, Washington on November 22, 1940. Olive Whiteman was born in New Orleans in December of 1909. She grew up in a privileged family, was spoiled by her parents, and, like all well to do girls in New Orleans, she was a debutante. Monroe Barrow Duffill was born in May of 1905 and likewise came from a well to do family.

Monroe's father was Harrison Mortimer Duffill, who was a retired Army Major. Tam's grandmother was Miriam Monroe. The grandparents divorced and his grandfather married Grandmother Lou.

Monroe, coming from a military background, also pursued a military career, but he chose the Navy instead of the Army. He attended the Annapolis Naval Academy and graduated in 1927. Spending his entire career in the Navy, he retired as a Rear Admiral. He was often away from the family and fought in the Korean War as well as World War II.

George Van Buren was a good friend of both Olive and Monroe. He spent a lot of time with the family—so much so that the boys called him "Unkie." George was always around. Olive, the two boys, and Unkie drove up to Maine every summer to stay at George's family lake home. The trips to Maine began in 1947 and continued till the boys were out of high school. Their father never went to Maine in the summer, and the boys loved this because they had the whole summer without their father's strictness and harsh punishment. They would stay most

of the summer there, and George's mother would join them. Brian and Tam have many great memories of fun times in Maine. They swam in the lake and made good friends with some local kids.

These trips to Maine with George did raise some eyebrows in the family because Monroe was absent. Some even believed that George might be Brian's father, but other relatives firmly said no, Monroe was definitely the father. When it came right down to it, no one will ever know, and both men were a big part of Brian's life. Unkie had even once saved Brian from drowning at Daytona Beach.

Growing up in this home, with Olive and Monroe as parents, was very difficult for Tam and Brian. They constantly felt that they were walking on eggshells, not knowing when one of their parents would explode. There was a constant atmosphere of fear. Not only was their father a strict disciplinarian, but he also had a drinking problem. Their father spanked the boys with a wooden coat hanger or a thick belt. When Olive got mad, she would slap them, and she would call Brian the "little bustard." At the dinner table, if they did not use correct manners, their knuckles would be hit with the heavy end of a dinner knife. If they didn't eat all their food, they were made to sit there until they did—sometimes for hours. Monroe would often be drunk and hit the boys and Olive for the least minor offense. Olive was sent to the hospital a few times after these beatings. Brian was the only one that he ever hit with a fist.

One evening, when Tam was sixteen years old and had become tall and muscular, he came in the house and found Duff, which was their father's nickname, beating up Brian and their mother. Tam came to their defense and threatened to hit Duff. A fight ensued, and Tam gave his father a good beating. He hit him so hard that Duff was bleeding from his nose and mouth. The others had to pull Tam off to stop the fight. After that, his father never hit him or anyone else in the family in front of him.

Tam trying to look cool like Elvis at age 16.

In many ways, Tam was the protector and guide for his younger brother, Brian. He taught Brian to ride a bike, to swim, play baseball, and drive a car, as well as keeping bullies away at school. Things like this, that their parents should have been doing, were done by Tam. As for Tam, he had to teach himself. The boys were often on their own.

As long as they stayed out of trouble, they were free to come and go as they pleased, within specified times. These freedoms led to much mischief. As a teenager, when the family was living in Virginia, Tam would sneak out of the house late at night and go for joy rides in the family car, a 1950 Mercury station wagon. He would meet friends to drag race. Once, Tam had to outrun the police when they were chasing him for drag racing in Mobile. Another time, Tam got caught by the police breaking into a house that was under construction. In 1956, after one too many infractions, Tam was sent to Hackley Boys School in White Plains, New York. He ran away from the school, and no one knew where he was for days.

When they were living in Virginia, the boys loved to go to baseball games at Griffith Stadium and watch the Washington Senators play. On Sundays, they would have Double Header Day. The boys would leave home about eleven AM, go by bus and street car to the stadium, and get home about 8:00 or 9:00 P.M. They were young kids, maybe middle school age, with no supervision, going from Arlington to Washington, D.C. This was a long distance, between large cities, but their parents didn't care as long as they stayed out of trouble. Once, they even missed a bus and walked sixty blocks through a not-so-safe area, but made it without any problems.

The family lived in Arlington, Virginia till 1957, and then moved, first to Mobile and then to Daphne, which is on the other side of Mobile Bay, in 1958. In Mobile, Tam had attended Murphy High School, and Brian attended a military school. Their father had tried to make Tam attend the military school, but when they sent him to take an entrance exam, Tam refused to even pick up the pen to take the test. He got his way and went to Murphy High.

In Daphne, both boys attended Fairhope High School. At that time, Tam had a 1955 Ford convertible that his father had bought for him so that he and Olive wouldn't have to run the boys around. This gave them a lot more freedom to get into trouble. Tam was still drag racing and almost got caught a few times.

At the young age of fourteen, Tam taught himself to play the guitar. He went to one guitar lesson and decided he just wanted to play by ear and learn on his own, figuring he didn't need to know how to read or write music. He had a band called "The Rebel Rockers," and they won a "Battle of the Bands" contest in 1959. For this they were named the "Best High School Band in Alabama."

Tam with his band, The Rebel Rockers.

Because Tam did not learn to read and write music, we do not have the music to almost all his songs. We have the lyrics he wrote, but the music was in his head. He never did record most of it or get someone to write the music for him. This is so unfortunate. I tried to remember the tunes to a few and write them, but had little success.

Tam loved animals all his life. When he was living in Virginia, he had two ducks named "Quackie" and "Wackie." He kept them in the basement and slept in the basement with them, letting them outside in the daytime.

One summer, when Tam came home from camp, he was told that his dog had run away and hadn't been found. He found out that his father had taken it to the pound, knowing that it would be put to sleep. Duff got rid of the dog because he just didn't like them. In high school, Tam had a small, nonpoisonous snake as a pet and took it to school with him several times. It was great fun scaring the girls, and showing it off to the boys.

He also loved old cars and motorcycles and had many through the years as a teenager and as an adult. He worked during the summers in Maine for a farmer that was near the lake cabin property of the Van Burens. One year he worked in the potato sheds in Alabama where they sorted and bagged potatoes. Earning his own money, he would save up and buy an old car.

In 1959 he bought a 1948 Harley motorcycle and drove it all the way from Maine to Alabama. His parents didn't know it till he pulled up in their driveway. He was allowed to keep it because they reasoned that if he could drive it all the way from Maine, he must be able to handle it, and he had paid for it himself.

Tam graduated from high school in 1959 and went to Montevallo College

Tam's 1948 Harley in 1961.

Senior picture, 1959.

in Alabama. With scholarships and summer jobs, Tam put himself through college. Because his college roommate could not see, Tam would take him out to a ball field, hold his hand, and run. This was the only way that a blind person could enjoy the exhilarating sensation of running. Tam was not concerned with how this might look to other people.

He met Joyce in college, and they married in 1963 when Tam graduated. She got pregnant, and Tam felt he had to do the right thing, even though he suspected that she might have gotten pregnant on purpose. They moved to Savannah, Georgia, in the fall of 1963, where he had gotten a job teaching. Barry, their son, was born that same year.

Montevallo College, Freshman year, L-R: Michael Hill, Harper Baddley, Tam Duffill.

The marriage to Joyce was not good for several reasons. Tam was too young to settle down and had many affairs during their marriage. Joyce must have also come from a violent childhood, because she started hitting Tam and slapping him when she would become angry. It was a recipe for trouble. Although Tam wanted to have the loving family life with Joyce and Barry that he did not have when he was growing up, it was doomed to failure. They separated in 1967 and divorced in 1968.

In Savannah, Tam was a very popular teacher that the students loved. When he grew a beard and the school wanted him to shave, the students stood up for him. At a meeting before the school board, Tam told them that  Jesus had a beard, and if it was good enough for Jesus, it should be OK for him. There was such a big deal made of this that the Savannah paper wrote an article about Tam and put his picture on the front page of the Sunday Magazine section. The title of the article was *"Troubadour of the Troubled,"* and told about his talent as a singer-guitarist playing in clubs around Savannah on weekends and teaching during the week.

In about 1965 or so, Joyce and Tam moved to Atlanta, and he got a job teaching in Jonesboro, Georgia. He began playing in clubs in Atlanta like The Bottom of the Barrel, The 12th Gate, The Bistro, and the Little Five Points Pub and became very popular. He had recorded a record back in 1961, with Groove Records, titled "Cooly Dooly," but it only sold about 5000 copies. He had spent the summer of 1961 driving around the South, stopping at radio stations, asking them to play his record. In Atlanta, he thought he was going to get a record contract with a local label, but it didn't pan out. However, many years after this, Tam was inducted into the Rockabilly Hall of Fame for "Cooly Dooly" and its flip side, "You Put The Hurt On Me." (See www.rockabillyhall.com/tamduffill.html)

Tam's page on Rockabilly Hall of Fame website.

On March 11, 1965, James Reeb, a white Unitarian minister, died after being attacked by a group of white supremacists in Selma, Alabama. He had come from Boston when Dr. King had asked ministers to support the nonviolent protest movement for voting rights in Alabama. Tam read about this, saw it on the news, and was deeply moved. He was so moved that his life was pulled in two new directions. He began going to the Unitarian Universalist Congregation of Atlanta, and, years later, he would become a founding member of the Unitarian Universalist Congregation of Marietta.

He was also inspired to quit his job teaching and work for Dr. Martin Luther King, Jr. at SCLC, "Southern Christian Leadership Council." This was in about 1967. He did continue to sing in clubs at night. Joyce was not too happy with this decision. The SCLC job was a volunteer job. Andrew Young hired Tam to run the Varityper. This was an oversized, special typewriter that was able to "justify," or align text, on the right edge, and was used for all SCLC's leaflets and pamphlets.

Donna Overall (Donna McBride at the time) was sent to SCLC to train Tam to use the Varityper. She had seen Tam perform at the clubs, but had never met him. While they were working, Dr. King came in, and they were privileged to meet him for the first time. Donna and Tam would become friends. As would happen with Donna and several other people Tam knew, there would be many years of no contact, and then they would find him again and renew the friendship just a few years before he died.

Working at SCLC was a dream job for Tam. He was very politically active and greatly admired Dr. King. He met him several times and recalls in some of his writing how Dr. King would greet him. "How are you doing Mr. Duffill?" On one occasion Tam asked him to sign one of his books, *Stride Toward Freedom,* which Dr. King graciously did. He recalled once going into King's office when no one was there and described this in his writing, telling how he felt to be there and what the office looked like.

Tam was working at SCLC when Dr. King was killed and describes in his writing, being at the funeral, telling how people were reacting, describing how the events were unfolding, and how he was feeling. His descriptions are vivid and really put you at the scene. He was very emotionally shaken by the loss of such a great man.

Two of Tam's greatest heroes were Dr. King and JFK. When Kennedy was shot on November 22, 1963, Tam was teaching in Savannah. A student came up to him and said "Mr. Duffill, do you know that our President has been shot?" This is how he found out about the tragedy. It was late in the day at school, and he was grateful for that because it was difficult to hide his grief. It was also Tam's birthday that day, which is something he never forgot. Even years after, birthday cake never tasted the same. He remembered hearing terribly racist remarks around Savannah in the days following Kennedy's death.

After Tam and Joyce separated in 1967, he moved up to a cabin on a lake in north Georgia. He was working at SCLC and singing in clubs around Atlanta on weekends. Most of his best writing was done during this time. It was a period of inward reflection and spiritual searching. The cabin was on a large piece of land, secluded and quiet. It had no heat or plumbing, and no TV, but it was the perfect environment for soul searching. His dog, his guitar, and a radio kept him company.

He felt much pain from the loss of the family he had hoped to have with Joyce and his son, Barry. Although much of this writing is positive and spiritual, some of it reflects his pain and disillusionment with the world and his situation. Tam was seeking the answers to all those important questions about life and its meaning. I think that he found some answers, but still had many questions.

Throughout the '60s, while Tam and Joyce were living in Atlanta, they were friends with Bud and Miki Foote. Bud was an English professor at Georgia Tech, and together Bud and Miki help found the Atlanta Folk Music Society.

Tam with old friend Miki (Foote) Davis.

In December of 1968, Miki heard from the police that they were taking Tam to Grady Hospital. She called Joyce, and they rushed to Grady, not knowing what had happened. Earlier that day, Tam had gone to Joyce's, and he took one of two pistols that he owned. When he left, he told Joyce, "Don't hold yourself responsible." She didn't know what he meant, but didn't think anything about it.

When Miki and Joyce got to the hospital, they were told that a passerby found Tam, slumped over the steering wheel of his VW van, in front of the Georgia Mental Health Institute gate. It looked like it might be an overdose. As the EMTs stopped for a moment to talk to Joyce, Miki looked closely at Tam and noticed a small round hole in his temple. Then they knew when she said, "He's shot himself."

The doctors told Joyce that if he made it through the first forty-eight hours or so, he might survive. They also said that if he survived he would probably be a vegetable for the rest of his life. No one could predict what disabilities he might be left with.

He had attempted suicide once before this, by taking a bunch of pills. Unsuccessful, he was sent to GMHI, Georgia Mental Health Institute. After being there for several months, he was released by his psychologist, only to shoot himself not long after being released. Tam and I happened to run into that same psychologist, years after, and he told Tam that he had felt much guilt and that he had obviously released him too early from GMHI. Tam assured him that he was not responsible.

Because Tam was a popular singer in Atlanta at this time, Bud Foote wrote an article about him shooting himself that was in *The Great Speckled Bird,* the local hippiedom paper at the time. Bud wrote under the name "Og King of Bashan," a character from the Torah and the Old Testament. *(See page 194 for this article.)*

A local artist sculpted a life-size nude of Tam, wearing only a peace symbol pendant, in a clear coffin and showed it at the Atlanta Arts and Crafts Festival in the spring. When the art piece didn't sell, and Tam had survived, the artist gave it to Tam. He named it "Lazarus," and he still had it when he moved in with me in 1979. We kept it for many years, but he finally let it go.

When someone attempts suicide, the question that always comes up is *why.* When I asked Tam this question, he said that there were several reasons. One was his failed marriage, and because Joyce was hitting and slapping him, he was afraid he would start hitting her back. This would put him right back in the same situation that he was in with his parents, but he would be doing the hitting and be no better than his father. He could not bear this.

Also, Bill Lowery, an Atlanta music producer, had Tam come into his studio for a recording session. Tam was very excited because he was led to believe he would get a contract; but this didn't happen. Additionally, his two biggest heroes, JFK and Dr. King, had both been gunned down—Dr. King only a few months before. Thus, Tam became disillusioned and depressed.

He had always been very sensitive and felt things more deeply than most people. This may have been because he was very intelligent. Before he shot himself, his IQ was about 145. After, it was about 100. If he hadn't started with a high IQ, he would have been retarded after "the bullet," which is how he referred to that suicide attempt.

When he was released from Grady Hospital, his mother took him back to her home in Alabama for him to recover from the gunshot. He had to learn to walk and to do everything again. This took months of physical and occupational therapy. Talking to me about the whole incident of "the bullet," he told me that he didn't remember shooting himself. The last thing that he remembered was leaving Joyce's house with the gun, and the first thing that he remembered after the incident was riding to Alabama in his mother's car.

After "the bullet," his visible handicaps were partial paralysis of his left little finger and some paralysis of his left foot. He also had invisible handicaps. He lost his short-term memory and much of his IQ. All the years we were married, Tam's memory loss was obvious. His long-term memory was still good. He could remember the words to songs he knew a long time ago and recount his childhood. He would often ask me to repeat something

I had just told him a few minutes before, due to short-term memory loss. One good thing was that he was not depressed anymore. The doctors said that the bullet went through the frontal lobe of the brain, and that is the same area that they give patients shock treatments to cure depression.

Although his injuries were substantial, he did recover and return to Atlanta to live on his own, and he could still play the guitar. He was able to get a job at Georgia State University Library, re-shelving books. Tam loved to read books. He would sometimes spend more time reading the books than putting them back on the shelves. He really liked this job, but, as you can imagine, it didn't last that long because of his lack of discipline. He would go from job to job until he finally was able to collect social security disability and receive help from his father.

While he was working at Georgia State University Library in the winter of 1971, he met Donna Stewart. The cool college kids hung out in The Refectory, and that is where Tam met Donna. She was immediately attracted to this handsome, blue-eyed bohemian and invited him to dinner. After that they spent a lot of time together.

Tam decided to move to Savannah after the job at Georgia State didn't work out. He kept in touch with Donna, and they would visit occasionally on weekends. The Nancy Hanks train ran between Atlanta and Savannah, so it was an easy way for them to travel between the two cities.

In the summer of 1971, Donna and Tam planned a trip

Tam in Heffalump, his VW van.

to Santa Fe in his VW van. He had painted it green with splotches of color. To make it look more conservative for the trip, they painted it primer gray and named it Heffalump, because it looked like a gray elephant. The van was made into a camper. It had a foldout bed and cabinets and a fold back roof door so you could see the sky. They enjoyed many trips in the van to places like Jekyll Island, the North Georgia mountains, North Carolina, New Mexico, and St. George Island, in Florida.

On one of their camping trips, Tam and Donna were sitting around a campfire with Tam playing the guitar and singing. People nearby at the campsite came over to join them and enjoy the music. Despite the age differences, the older people seemed to like it. One older man was deaf and asked if he could put his hand on the guitar to "hear" the music. Tam, of course, said yes, and the man seemed to enjoy the music as much as everyone else.

Tam moved back to Atlanta and moved in with Donna in a small apartment across from Piedmont Park. He had an agent for a while who got him a few jobs singing in small bars around town and once at the student center at North Georgia College in Dahlonega, Georgia.

The 1948 Martin guitar, that Tam had since he was a teenager, was always with him when he and Donna went to visit friends. He never tired of playing and singing, and always carried with him a small, pocket size notebook and pen to write down ideas for songs and poems. He was constantly writing, even sometimes on napkins at restaurants.

Although he wrote many songs, when Tam sang in public, he always sang songs written by other people because his songs were not protected by copyright. He would share the background and the history of the songs he sang and their writers with the audience. His extensive knowledge of music was impressive, as well as his large collection of albums.

A few years after "the bullet," Tam performed in public less and less. He played in bands that would get together and practice regularly, but it was mainly for fun and not for any serious prospects. He did continue to enjoy playing for friends.

Tam had a grand mal seizure only a few months after he and Donna had been living together. After she called 911, he was taken to Grady Hospital. The doctors said that he would be prone to seizures for the rest of his life because of the head injury caused by the bullet. He was put on Phenobarbital medication to prevent seizures and would have to take it daily from then on.

Drifting apart in their relationship, Tam and Donna finally went their separate ways in about 1975, but continued to be friends and have friends in common for many years. Donna met her second husband, Hal, at a small community church in Little Five Points that she had been invited to visit by Tam.

Donna and Tam renewed their friendship in 2012, after thirty years of no contact. By then, he was living in the assisted living home, and Donna visited him as often as she could until his death.

Around 1977, when Tam was riding his motorcycle on Ponce de Leon Avenue in Atlanta, a car hit him, and he was badly injured. Both bones were broken in his left, lower leg. The doctors wanted to amputate it, but Tam would not let them. After several surgeries, his leg was saved, but it left him with a limp and a brace he would have to wear for the rest of his life.

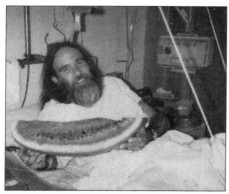
Tam after a car hit him on his motorcycle on Ponce de Leon Avenue.

As I have already told you, I met Tam in 1979. When I introduced him to my family, they did not like him at all. I had called one of my sisters to tell her about Tam. I asked her not to tell our mother, that I would do that soon enough. Because I had told her he had long hair, a full long beard, several tattoos, and that he was disabled, she immediately went to my mother and told her. "Thanks a lot," was all I had to say to my sister.

About those tattoos: the first one Tam got was in

Savannah in the early '60s, on his ankle, and it simply said TRUTH. Later, he got more tattoos that were larger and more visible on his arms. One of these was a snake and a panther entwined in a battle, which he said represented his parents. Another was a skeleton on a motorcycle, which was himself. The third was a skull with a snake crawling out of it, which I think represented himself again with all his mental struggles.

My whole family told me that I was making a big mistake, that Tam was not good enough for me. "You need a man who can care for you, not a man that you will have to care for." My mother called Tam several times while I was at work trying to talk him into leaving me. She told him that I had a serious kidney condition and that he would never be able to pay the doctor bills. Also, she offered to give him $10,000 if he would leave. I finally told my mother that if she made me choose between her and Tam, that she would never see me again, and I meant it. My whole family finally came around after many years—even my mother.

Christmas with my family.

We got married on July 15, 1980, exactly one year to the date that we met. A minister from Crawford Long Hospital married us at a park on the campus of Emory University.

No one was present but two friends of Tam's, who were our witnesses. For our honeymoon, we went to Lake Lanier and stayed at a motel for the weekend.

Those first two years we were together, we were inseparable. I can remember once, when we were going to follow his son somewhere, Barry wanted one of us to ride with him. Since we couldn't stand to be apart, we chose to ride together and follow him. I'm sure his son thought we were crazy, but we were madly in love. Several people at work even guessed, because they would say to me, "You are glowing; you must be in love."

When we first got together, I did try to reunite Tam and his son. They had been estranged for years. Joyce had done nothing but tell Barry bad things about his father. Now he was old enough to drive and could sneak away from her to visit us. This only lasted a short time. Barry went up north to a private school that Tam's father paid for. Duff, Tam's father, was living in Boston and wanted to get to know his grandson.

Also, Joyce had Barry change his last name to her present husband's name. This, again, marked a break in the relationship, and we didn't see Barry any more. Tam was deeply hurt by the fact that Barry changed his last name.

We had very little money and lived from paycheck to paycheck. I was still working at Crawford Long Hospital, and Tam was on Social Security disability, which didn't pay much because he had only worked as a teacher for a few years. We were living in a house on Fernwood Circle in Brookhaven, in Atlanta. The house had a basement and an upstairs apartment. I had taken over the whole house when Nancy moved to Colorado. To make ends meet, we had sublet the upstairs for the rent of the whole house, which was $235 a month. Even though we had a free place to live, we still barely survived.

The basement had concrete floors, no shower, and was very small. When it rained very hard for a long time, it would flood and there would be an inch or so of water all over the living room floor. Once, when Barry came over to visit, it was flooded. I was so embarrassed for him to see how we were living. Slugs would also get into the basement, so you couldn't walk around barefooted because you might step on one. Despite all this, we were in love, so it didn't matter.

We didn't know that we would soon face some very hard times. I decided to go back to school to get a higher nursing degree. I had to continue to

Our first winter together.

work and go to school at the same time. Nursing school is extremely demanding and difficult. I didn't get enough sleep for two years and became very run down. Toward the end, one of my teachers took me aside and told me that I looked like walking death and maybe I should consider dropping out of school. This was a hard decision for me to make. If I didn't get through school so I could earn more income, Tam and I would be living in poverty forever. However, I did finally drop out.

In about 1983, Tam's Social Security Disability was challenged. They made us prove that he was still disabled and needed disability income. This was right in the middle of the time I was back in school, from 1982 to 1984. I had to go with Tam to doctor visits and appointments with the lawyer because of his short-term memory loss. They had him retested by a psychologist and medical doctor. Then we had to go to court for the judge's decision. Thankfully, he decided that Tam was still disabled. We were poor enough without losing the disability income.

Tam cut his hair because of the Social Security challenge and Joyce suing him.

It was just after I had dropped out of nursing school, that Barry was a senior in high school and getting ready to go to college. Duff had died in May of 1982, and Tam had inherited a small amount of money. Joyce sued Tam for back child support. We met with our lawyer and Joyce with her lawyer to settle. Since Tam could not prove that he had paid child support, he had to give her $8,000. During that meeting, if looks could kill, Tam would have been dead. Joyce glared at him through the entire meeting. I have never seen so much hate in anyone's face.

Not long after this was settled, Joyce sued us again. She wanted Tam to pay for Barry's college expenses. She had a letter from Duff stating that he would pay for Barry's college. She wanted that money taken out of Tam's inheritance. Since a letter does not supersede a will, we won that lawsuit.

Around 1984, because of all the stress of working, school, and two lawsuits, I had a nervous breakdown. I was in therapy for two years. I can remember being so depressed that I started crying because I couldn't open a bottle of ketchup. Tam and I weathered all this together, and all the stress only made us closer. It was us against the world, and we were united.

With the inheritance from Duff, Tam and I bought a lot in a trailer park in Acworth, Georgia, and a used trailer for $3,000. After dropping out of nursing school, I had gone back to work full time at Crawford Long Hospital. This was a thirty-five mile commute to work for me, but we had gotten out of that miserable house in Atlanta, and had a place of our own.

After we had lived there for a few years, Tam's mother gave us enough to buy the empty lot next to us, and a brand new, furnished single wide trailer to put on it. This was the best place that we had ever lived.

In May of 1985, Tam's stepfather died and left him a trust fund, from which he received a monthly income. This boosted our income enough that I was able to stop

Visiting Tam's mother.

working at Crawford Long. My last day at CWL was on March 6, 1986.

Tam bought a used BMW motorcycle. At that time, we were renting the old trailer next door that we used to live in, to some friends, David and Gail. They also had a motorcycle. We would ride the bikes up into the north Georgia mountains on day trips together. This lasted until Tam had a fall on the bike. Although he wasn't injured, he decided to sell it. The risk of being badly hurt again wasn't worth it. He sold the bike on April 11, 1986, to Gene, an old friend who he hadn't seen in years and who just happened to see the ad in the paper.

In May of 1994, Tam's mother died and left him another trust. We were in better shape financially than we had ever been. We were finally able to buy our first house. After living in rundown apartments and trailers, this was really exciting. We found a house for sale only a mile or so from where we were living.

It was a little less than three acres with a ranch style house, a barn, and a fenced-in pasture. I had horses when I was a kid, so I was thrilled to be able to again. We bought the house, two horses, and Tam bought a 1934 Ford Coupe. It was a beautiful car and looked brand new, because it was a kit car, yellow with black interior. Tam loved that car, and we attended many car shows.

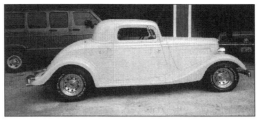
Tam's 1934 Ford Coupe.

We were living the good life in most ways, but there was a monkey on our backs. We had both been smoking grass for many years. I only smoked one or two joints at night to go to sleep and occasionally during the day, on special occasions. Tam smoked as much as he could get and afford, every day—usually ten joints a day. This was the case for the seventeen years we were together, until I quit smoking on March 30, 1996.

His mother had been giving us large gifts of money every Christmas for several years before she died. This was great, but also bad because it made it possible for Tam to smoke more and more. I couldn't stop him. Marijuana was our drug of choice; we didn't do any hard drugs.

We didn't know it at the time, but smoking grass was damaging our health—my kidney and Tam's lungs. I was born with only two thirds of one kidney which functions correctly. The other parts of my kidneys have very few filtering units and don't do anything. I quit smoking that March because I was having kidney problems, and my doctor told me that I would be on dialysis if I didn't quit smoking. This was enough to motivate me to quit.

I tried to get Tam to quit, but he refused. He didn't believe me when I told him that he was damaging his lungs. He would not quit until about 2002 when he was in the hospital with lung problems, and a doctor told him that he had to quit if he wanted to live. His damaged lungs eventually led to him having to move into an assisted living facility and be on oxygen.

Tam's 1946 Ford Coupe.

Our time living at our house in Acworth, before our health problems, was great. I enjoyed my horses, and Tam enjoyed his cars. Not only did he have the '34 Ford, he also had a blue 1946 Ford Coupe and a 1975 Mustang.

I stayed with Tam for two years after I quit smoking, but, as you can imagine, it was very hard to be drug free and live with someone that was constantly smoking grass. I can remember riding in the car with him smoking and me with my head out the window trying not to inhale second-hand smoke.

Things came to a head on my fiftieth birthday, in 1998. I had invited two couples to come over for dinner that night. I ask Tam not to smoke because I didn't want the house to smell like pot. Since he couldn't smoke, he had several drinks of Jack Daniels and was so drunk that he couldn't come to the dinner table. I was so embarrassed; I had to make up an excuse to our guests for why he couldn't come to the dinner table. That was the straw that broke the camel's back. Sadly, it was the end of our relationship. He moved into the bedroom on the other side of the house. Three months later, I moved into a house down the street that I bought with money from an inheritance from my mother, who had died on August 30, 1997. We stayed married for another two and one-half years, living in separate houses just a few yards down the street from each other.

About one year after living separately, I began dating Chris, my current husband, and Tam was dating a waitress named Pam. Within a short time, Chris was living with me, and Pam was living with Tam. Six months into our relationship, Chris asked me to get a divorce, so I began the process. It took a year and a half for the divorce to be final because of Tam's disability. The court appointed a lawyer for him, to protect his interest, and I hired a lawyer for myself. It was a friendly divorce. I even took Tam to his appointments with his lawyer. Both our lawyers were amazed at how friendly the divorce was. Tam and I continued to see each other on a regular basis and remained friends.

Pam had two sons that were young adults. When Tam told me that they were going to move in with him and Pam, I advised him against it. Only two years later, Pam died, and her drug addict sons began harassing Tam. At one point, they pulled a gun on Tam and demanded his money and pot. After they left, Tam called me and I picked him up and hid him in the house we used to live in. We swapped cars so Pam's sons wouldn't know he was there, and I gave him my cell phone.

Tam called me the next day and said he was having trouble breathing, so Chris and I went to get him and take him to the hospital. The doctors told him that if he wanted to live he had to stop smoking. I called Brian and told him what was going on, so he came up from Montrose, Alabama. Then, Brian and I moved Tam out of his house into Dogwood Forest, an assisted living home. There he would be safe from Pam's sons, but not alone. I always worried about Tam living alone because he had seizures. If no one found him in time, he could die from the seizures with no medical treatment.

Although he was forced to stop smoking at this time, the damage had already been done to his lungs, and he did end up on oxygen. His health slowly deteriorated over the next ten years. During these last years, he had only about twenty percent lung function.

During those last ten years of his life at the assisted living place, he made friends, had a girlfriend or two, and sang in the lobby every Tuesday at 2:00 P.M. Many of those Tuesdays I would come over to hear him sing. I visited him regularly and had dinner in the dining room with him many times. Brian also visited him as often as he could.

Several old friends reconnected with Tam and came to visit him when they were able. This included two old girlfriends, Donna Stewart and Myra Skipper, Donna Overall, who had trained him at SCLC so many years before, and Brooks Hunnicutt, a fellow musician and singer who had a long career as a backup singer in Los Angeles. He was very popular with the staff and residents of Dogwood Forest.

Tam and Brooks Hunnicutt.

When I woke up on the morning of January 2, 2014, I had a message from Dogwood Forest and one from Brian. The messages were sent very early that morning. This could only mean one thing—Tam was in trouble. I thought that he was probably in the hospital again with a hip joint replacement out, or that he had fallen again. I had been with him the night before, and sat with him while he ate dinner in his room because he didn't feel well enough to go to the dining room. He was fine when I left him that night.

I called the assisted living home first. They told me that they had found him on the floor in the bathroom unresponsive and called an ambulance. When they told me that he hadn't made it, that he was gone, I couldn't believe it. The last thing that I said to him was, "I'll see you in the morning," and he thanked me for coming.

I called Brian, and he said he would be coming in a few days. He asked me to go to Tam's apartment and collect whatever I thought was valuable or sentimental and take it to my house. This was very difficult for me, but I was able to do it. I collected Tam's guitars and other keepsakes.

The funeral was on January 8, 2014, in Acworth, Georgia, at Collins Funeral Home, and Tam was buried in Acworth. Georgia had become his home many years before, and his roots were there, not in Alabama.

The day Brian was cleaning out Tam's place after the funeral, Donna Overall came by. Thank goodness she did, because she discovered the notebooks Tam had been writing in for the last forty-five years.

Tam and Donna Overall.

Brian gave Tam's cassette tape collection to Donna. Among these tapes, she discovered a cassette of Tam playing and singing from 1968. It is the only recording that we have of Tam from this time.

After reading through Tam's journals, I decided to put this book together. Brian generously allowed me to keep Tam's writings long enough for me to compile the book. I thought his writing was beautiful and that he deserved to be remembered, if not by the world, at least by his friends and family. He was extremely talented, when you consider that almost everything he wrote was a first draft. The words flowed out with such apparent ease. He was able to express himself so poetically. Very few people can write like that.

You can see a big difference in his writing from 1967 through 1968, before "the bullet," and his writing after "the bullet," from 1969 to 2014. I have already explained how he started with a very high IQ and ended with an average IQ. The quality of his writing progressively declined through the years as he smoked more and more grass. He just didn't possess the brilliance he had before he shot himself. However, he never quit writing. I think it was a great outlet for him and a way to say things he couldn't otherwise say to any one else.

Another great favor Donna Overall has done for us is that she recorded Tam playing and singing at Dogwood Forest in July of 2011 and posted the videos to her YouTube channel. To find these recordings, just go to YouTube.com and do a search for Tam Duffill.

Tam left so much for us. My hope is that he will be remembered.

—Marianne Duffill Cox

Tam Knew Talent

Tam knew and performed with a number of talented people during his life. Good musicians always recognize other talented people. There was Ray Whitley, who wrote several hits for the group "The Tams." They were friends for many years.

Barry Etris, whose beautiful words about Tam are on the back cover of this book, knew Tam well. They were really good friends and often jammed together at The Bistro, one of Atlanta's favorite folk clubs.

Another '60s friend of Tam's was Brooks Hunnicutt. She had a long career as a backup singer for musicians such as Stephen Stills, Rod Stewart, Kris Kristofferson, Steve Cropper, Mac Davis, Bobby Womack, Kenny Rogers, Loretta Lynn, John Prine, Molly Hatchet, David Cassidy, and Helen Reddy. She also recorded her own CD in 2013, entitled *Out of the Shadows*.

An Atlanta favorite in the 1960s was Jeff Espina. He and Tam performed together, and occasionally backed each other up. Jeff, who served as a Ship's Captain in the Merchant Marine for many years, remembers Tam with great fondness.

In his later years, in the early 2000s, when he was living in Acworth, GA, Tam got to know the retired drummer for Lynyrd Skynyrd, Bob Burns. Bob died in a car accident on April 3, 2015, in Cartersville, Georgia.

Some old friends remember Tam...

John Caparisos, right, was half of the Savannah duo, "Pete and John."

I met Tam at a Hootenanny on a Saturday afternoon in 1964 at Ye Olde Crow's Nest in Savannah, Georgia. The Folk Era was still in full bloom, and everyone seemed to play the guitar. We were all so young then. The group I was in, "The Whalers," played a few songs. Tam was the first to greet us after the performance and offered us praise and encouragement. That meant a lot. He gave a thumbs up to the owner, and we began playing on the weekends when Tam took his breaks. After a year our trio became a duo, "Pete and John." We sang on the same stage Tam did for around two and a half years.

Tam was a mentor to me way back then. His singing and playing talents seemed endless. He never looked down on anyone but always had kind words for everyone. At that time Tam was singing at the Crow's Nest a couple of nights a week and on weekends. The crowds loved him and came from other cities to hear him. One of Tam's enduring qualities was his ability to make one feel like the only person on earth. His words were always gentle, punctuated by his wonderful laugh.

I considered Tam a friend. We had many coffees together before many shows, and often talked during breaks. The Crow's Nest was like Tam's world, and we were proud to share it. As life would have it, my singing partner, Peter Polites, and I graduated from high school and went off to college. Tam moved on, and I lost track of him.

Decades later, I discovered his whereabouts and called him immediately. I was amazed that he remembered me! We talked several times, and I sent him a copy of "Save Savannah!", a CD of original tunes my old friend and singing partner Peter and I had written and recorded. I was very happy to hear how much he liked our music!

Our few conversations took me back to memories of the Crow's Nest and Tam's kindness. They reminded me of Tam's excellent performances of the music he loved on the stage he enjoyed so much. It was my honor to know him. I'll never forget Tam, his music, and above all, his friendship.

—Fr. John A. Caparisos, Col, USAF (ret)
  St. Paul's Greek Orthodox Church, Savannah, Georgia

I think the first time I heard him must have been at the Crow's Nest in 1964 (just off Broughton Street in Savannah). A steep flight of stairs led down to a dirt-floored basement with about eight tables, a tiny stage and a bare lightbulb hanging above the performer. Tam was still teaching history and civics to junior high kids… Married to Joyce and new father of Barry. He was my best man when I got married to Jeanne in 1965. We all went to Anna's Little Napoli for spaghetti and chianti that evening. I so loved that man. Will until I die.

—*Barr Nobles*
  Clearwater, Florida

Tam Duffill: a gentle and soft-spoken man, devoid of conceit, with a smile that I remember as "disarming." Tam sat in with me in the late '60s, at the Bottom of the Barrel, and the early '70s, in Underground Atlanta, where we were performing at different clubs. It was always a pleasure to hear his tambourine holding a jangling beat under our music.

—*Jeff Espina*
  Palm Harbor, Florida

I met Tam back in the old coffee house days in Atlanta. I very much enjoyed the music he made and regretted that I didn't get to know him better before I fled to San Francisco in order to avoid my parents' ongoing World War III post-divorce antics.

After being in Los Angeles for a number of years, I planned a trip back home to visit my family in Atlanta. At that time, I was singing as a professional for whoever would pay my bills—from such esteemed artists as Stephen Stills and Rod Stewart to Kenny Rogers and Mac Davis—and doing every other musical thing I could to make money.

A few days before I flew to Atlanta, I heard that Tam had tried to *(Cont'd)*

Brooks Hunnicutt, Stephen Stills.

commit suicide by shooting himself in the temple. My friends told me he was in Grady Hospital, had been running high fevers, and it was feared that he wouldn't live. This may sound strange, but I got this "message," a repeating thought came into my mind, that I should get off the plane in Atlanta, put my bags down in the front hall of my mother's house and immediately take a cab to Grady. How strange!!! This thought persisted and was all I could think about as I packed, flew, and landed in Atlanta, whereupon I did indeed, put my bags down in the front hall of my mother's house and immediately take a cab to Grady.

I had never been to Grady (more commonly known in those days as, "The Gradys") and felt totally intimidated at the size of the place and the maze I went through to find Tam. He was in a large ward and had a tracheotomy so he couldn't talk. I wasn't sure what he could understand as he looked up, wide-eyed and unable to speak, but I reintroduced myself as an acquaintance from the past and began speaking. I don't remember what I said that day, but I do remember holding both of his hands tightly and telling him that it wasn't his time to leave and that he had to fight. It was probably a very short visit, but it felt as though I had spoken to him for a long, long time. His bright eyes never left my face. When I finished speaking, I was freezing cold and shivering. I went to my Mom's house and slept until the next day. That night Tam's fever broke, and he began his road to recovery. I didn't see him again for over 40 years.

When I next saw Tam, he came to a Pickers' Circle at Cowboy's BBQ restaurant in Covington, Georgia, and it was a true delight to see his fragile countenance enter the room. He walked ever so carefully and bent over, but the bright eyes and great smile were still present from years before. That was the beginning of a rekindled friendship. He wasn't up to singing that night, but he later came to the Downwind Restaurant at the Peachtree DeKalb Airport and got up and performed a few songs to the great delight of many old friends who were in attendance.

Donna Overall and I took Tam to dinner a few years back, and it was a thoroughly delightful evening. His deep, subtle sense of humor always made me laugh and feel wonderful. I regret that I didn't have more opportunities to spend time with Tam recently because his indomitable spirit was a joy to be around.

—*Brooks Hunnicutt, Singer, Musician*
  Shady Dale, Georgia

Meditations

Dedicated to
> *Neal*

Who lost his job one night
> *Joyce*

Who so loved and was hurt
> *Tom*

Whose gentle butt was drafted
> *Gene*

Who is a patriarch of sorts
> *John*

Who owns a bookstore
> *Bruce*

Who runs a church coffeehouse
> *Terry*

Who runs a folk nightclub
> *And God*

Who showed me His face in a dream

Day's Guide

A Rise
B Have coffee, nuts, and fruit
C Read one to three hours
D Do exercises 45 minutes
E Meditate and write, one to four hours (outdoors whenever possible)
F Eat lunch
G Nap, rest, or preferably take a walk or work on music
H Evening meal
I Read or visit or go to make necessary money by singing
J To sleep alone or with a lover
K Cycle is complete

So Easy

It is the easiest
most perfect
thing in the world
to write out whatever
you think and feel.
It is a beautiful thing
not to force it
or rewrite it.
Just put it down
at the point of inspiration
and let it lie,
to be barren
or be fertile.
Is it the field under the plow
that makes judgments?

Iron Creek

My son and I at Iron Creek, Suwanee, Georgia,
our little Amazon basin;
clear stream in woods unfolding adventures,
as we sail little boats down the still waters,
toward the rapids downstream.
We wonder which boat will make it.
Be mine—excited, we even place bets,
secretly on the other's boat.

My Innermost Thoughts

You want to read this?
You are reading it
or listening to it.
You are sharing my innermost thoughts
which I reveal only at inspiration
from day to day in meditation
after Hatha yoga exercises have been done.
Make an effort to span the gap
and get into my head.
These are not just words;
try to FEEL and UNDERSTAND
and LOVE and know I am separate
and yet so much you.

The God We Are

We must be made aware
   of the god
       we are
   the Lord
       within
the spirit in all
    living creatures
the
   oneness we can never
   fully proclaim as the
   divine animals we are
though we can become one with
   this oneness
through meditation, prayer and
     communion
         outdoors
              alone with nature and God around.

I Am Grateful *Tuesday, December 19, 1968*

Warm and rainy off and on,
drops on the lake
the cabin is secure.
I am so grateful.
Sit
quiet and listen to your
voice,
your sacred sanctum.
Deep within
listen to the knowing
denier
of the I.Q.
seeker
of the thou shalt
know.

The Wasp

A huge wasp sat down, alighted on my porch,
walks around and toward me.
A test,
a living creature,
a threat.
Fear…sit still.
He approaches slowly
to three inches,
I'm afraid.
Shall I squash him with my copy of
"The Tibetan Book of the Dead"?
He is alive.
He stops, bends his innocent head
and proceeds to dutifully clean his antenna
with miniature toothpick paws.
Forty-five seconds,
stops, quivers.
I flinch back.
He maneuvers to the east on another runway
and takes off toward the rising sun.

The Cross

In the trees
above the porch
a sturdy elm branch
sending two horizontal
branch brothers out,
so that a four way crossroads
intersection is formed,
as well as a cross.

The Rain Droplet

A drop of rain
   on a single leaf
   which the dark
bark
forms a
backdrop.
It forms,
grows heavy,
sagging.
A giant clear
pearl from above,
like the spike
gleaming from
the open dark
palm on the cross.
It drops just as I shift my eyes.
Behold it is gone…
but another has formed…
        grown ripe,
        shed its fruit,
        and given life.

To Walk Barefoot

To walk
barefoot
through the wet leaves
toward the lake,
get there,
wash hands,
soap suds
and then face
with wet cloth
cold from December
north Georgia waters.
Ah…
why don't you know
that by going back,
you go forward?

The Cabin

Our woods cabin
no TV, no plumbing,
no one around,
but got electricity
a good radio
a fender guitar
and my dog.

We are all potential Messiahs

Have faith
   that God will send
   helpers,
   brothers,
   Disciples,
knowing we are all potential Messiahs.

Let It Grow

The hair length
is not necessarily
the big thing.
Let it grow.
Never cut it voluntarily.
Never defeat yourself.
Make them lose something
with the clipping shears
they grip
to sizzer you into
submission.

Love God

Love I God
    and life
        and Divinity.

How To Be Immortal

I have been dead
    once before,
for a millennium,
and knew not
and suffered not
and I shall be again.
Live
prepared to die.
Give
yourself to something
bigger
better
more lasting—
a more loving world.
Turn on
others to the Spirit,
to love,
and you live on
immortal.

The Holy Beacon

The shimmering sun shaft
upon the brown
waters
is a holy beacon,
    guided light,
from my head
to the sun
and back again.

The Hawk

A huge hawk drifts below
the white pillow clouds
into the blue sky.
I follow him,
eyes glued.
Spirit up there,
riding the wind with him.
Almost, I am him, for a moment.
Flapping powerful wings
just once in a long distance.
Slow motion before crossing
behind the pine horizon.
Carry my spirit oh hawk
to the discoveries and the discoverers.

Learn and Grow

I have the feeling that
everything that happens
good or bad
is God's will.
It is an experience to grow upon.
A test, so that you
more fully know
    yourself
    your limits
    your strengths
    your divinity
and grow from it.
Learn and grow closer to
the Supreme Ground of Being.

Evening Fire *December 24, 1967*

Eve fire,
lick
fingers of fire,
shimmering
their essence
to give us heat
against
the first real
cold of December.
By
morning you will
be dying ashes.
Do your thing
tonight then,
and heat my fingers
to say your words.

Christmas Tree Balls *December 27, 1967*

Wet damp day
sitting on the couch
on the porch.
Sun breaks through
every once in a while,
exposing thousands
of crystal water droplets,
dangling
like miniature
Christmas tree balls
from naked dogwood branches.

*Knowing the truth with your brain and
knowing the truth with your Being, are
two very different things.*

*Reached a blackout cosmic consciousness level
three times today.*

*Thank you God. Your yogic energy charge to
the head brings you there.*

*I know the way now. I just need strength and
faith in myself and God to stay on the path,
walking and not sitting down afraid.*

I Am Free *Sunday January 7, 1968*

Now at last I am free to follow the Spirit.
The path is through the forest now, past the jungle
and is climbing the meadow over which
the mountain towers, overshadowing the flowers.
The Spirit is first and the mountain is the spirit.
The ascent beckons, the height challenges you
to the void above.
The top is within reach.
Very few reach it, few attempt it, and few acknowledge it.
Of the many, they are unaware.
Why are you blind?
Why do you not give it thought?
Why do you not climb,
or stop part way up and quit?
Why are those who have been to the top
unable to tell the rest of us?
If they do, why do we not hear?
Who are the deaf among us?
Why are so many of those few crest conquerors crucified?

I Fall Naked

I fall naked once again before the window
and see shadows of your soul,
fleeting on streams of consciousness
as dust flakes miniscule upwards
in the aimless sun.
Whose house do I stalk around?
The shell seems empty,
yet I hear heart beats
booming in the night, breathing regular.
For what purpose prowling about,
peering in with dusty eyeglasses and a stained mind.

Who of Us

Who of us can return to correct bathroom errors,
    closet mistakes of temper?
I have wondered too long about my head
    and its ego divinity,
that is only a shadow on the mirror, never held
    nor grasped nor understood.
Only glimpsed occasionally from some brief dark alleys
    where I pen myself at midnight.

The Circle *February 16, 1968*

The circle moves toward completion.
The law must be obeyed.
Honesty is carrying as few illusions as possible.

Those of Faith

We have all been dead once before.
Before the womb we suffered not.
Before saving ourselves we suffered much.
Being saved we know the second death to come is painless.
Fear is alien to those of faith.

I Have Visions

Something is dying in me.
I have visions of my corpse
in the earth, no box.
Staring upward eyes closed, peaceful.
Friends gathered around.
I watch above it all, wanting them to laugh
and have a party.
It was nice to be here for a while,
but death is painful and frightening,
is a pit you have to climb out of,
to return from, to come back somehow.
But something is being born.
While childbirth is painful,
I feel the Light.

I Am a Fool

I tell you I am a fool and a madman
and know no difference, have no choice,
am never sure if I can come back from insanity.
It is so attractive and exciting and fulfilling;
yes rewarding and challenging too.

A Star Shines

A star shines for you in the heavens.
There is no difference between
its glitter and your glitter,
but you are so much warmer
though I can hold you
no longer than I can the star.

Fallen From Grace

Having fallen from grace
to the highest level of outcast
the freest form of fortune
I let you know where I am in an instant
before going someplace else.

Fall Is Coming

Falling leaves, crescent shapes,
heart malingerer to a better time
and earlier spring, when all was birth.
Sunshine was rampant
and the innocent eyes,
those gentle veins of chlorophyll turn to brown
gathering in the forest
a foreknowledge of what is to come.

Naked Soul

Lying in the sun, naked soul
bare to the essentials
exposed to the world.
I have nothing to hide
but my insanity.

Days Float By *February 27, 1968*

White puffs giving the pine tops an upstream motion.
Floating by on lambs' paws silently,
the day moves by, another and another.
I wait not really caring for what,
mainly just floating along.
In the backdrop blue,
the wind's blunder
the sun's interruption.

My Cross

The cross I wear around my neck
is just a representation of one of God's religions.
They are all His.
I wear it because it speaks to the majority
of the people around me
in terms they can understand.
I know what it means to me.

The Drama of Life

Every moment of life a vast drama,
vast huge screenplay, Technicolor.
Don't know the ending.
Drama acted out with us in it,
playing a starring role.
And all those supporting cast of characters
held in the wings, waiting for a cue
to enter your stage, say and do their bit,
and split to leave you alone on stage at curtain time.

Eloise

I feel your presence in the woods around me
through the trees and tiny rain droplets.
You wander the hills and trod the wet
collecting magi wise woman gifts, leaves to deposit
inside our warm room of restoration.
Even now you bring home color filled leaves
now I thought were no more.
No one finds them but you
with frozen crystal ball droplets
clinging their temporary assault to hold beauty.
Picking up leaf wreaths to halo your
turquoise bonnet in thorns and texture.
Admonishing the dogs not to fight, to be friends.
Even pleading, coaxing Gene's cat to stop
tormenting the birds caught in their cage.
Listening to my pain, accepting my attempted
love gestures with seeing eyes.
You return from your woods tromp
and indeed there are gifts.
Sit down beside me on the porch
to watch the rain pelt the lake
in miniature volcanic indentions
that flatten out before we can hold it.
We love it that way.
Not a word to say—they are not necessary.
We hold hands, free to be alone in our oneness.

Martin's Death

How God loves his praise.
To put such soul in his people.
Listen soul my soul to heaven with his spirit.
Oh to be such a MAN.
And we all loved to be like him.
Please, just one prayer today,
as they let you return to earth
cycle completed.
Been to the top of the mountain
had visions, dreams, a prophet.
On Wednesday last, of his own death
died the next night.
Great man I tell you.
Penetrating wisdom, wise.
What is it to be nonviolent?
Thirteen years walked unafraid.
He trusted in God alone.
Dreamed a dream,
worked for, inspired hope
God lights a torch of love
love all men, even his enemies
want freedom for them too.
Legacy of love he left to his brothers.
Your dream is now ours,
to carry your torn march unto brotherhood.

April 4, 1968

Bless you life holding me together
somehow,
my mind flowing
gentle
again like April raindrops.
Gray day
following no dream.
Be desireless, they tell me
in loud shouts
which few can hear.

Worked for SCLC under another in Atlanta, his home.
I quit that September and went back to teaching in Jonesboro.
Sociology and encouraged them to question everything.

The Funeral

Thousands of people wait.
He belongs to them.
The mule train takes his body from there,
now back to the church.
His wife, black veiled,
requests tape of his last sermon
to be played now.
Oh God can I listen;
can I listen?
He talks of his own funeral.
"Tell 'em not to talk too long,
don't mention Nobel prize.
Just mention he tried
to give love to somebody.
He tried to feed the hungry.
He tried, he tried
to love justice, peace, righteousness,
to make a new world."
From his own funeral,
his words echo.
Black women crying in pews.
I cry here, dropping tears on this page.
You who died a martyr
on Calvary cross, in Memphis,
the Roman spear, a hotel window.
Who shot? Was it Judas or Pilate or racism, fear, hatred?

They're going to Morehouse,
after body placed on mule train.
He died—so stupid.
Lord made all,
even those of different color.
Chimes ring out,
casket being moved down aisle,
beautiful flowers
going outside church.
All politicians there,
US flag, flag of the church, UN flag on coffin,
carrying him down steps.
Many are praying, bowed heads,
casket adjusted on cart
drawn by two brown Georgia mules.
Crowds four abreast all around church
all last night to see him.
Widow leans on arms,
can't walk with casket.
One of her children by her,
heavily veiled.
Family not going to march with casket;
they all wait to follow.
Casket leaves with mules.
We are waiting; though we know
you have gone,
you are still with us forever
through the ages.
Thank you for this man of God, Lord.
Amen.

SCLC

Remember the guitar jam sessions
in the basement office on Auburn Avenue?
I wonder if he heard us ever
in his office on the ground floor.
Though he wasn't in very much,
when he arrived, the whole staff,
both floors got excited.
Word passed, "he's here."
He came in a real hero to us.
Knew where he was going.
Even said "how do you do Mr. Duffill?"
When he met me
and signed "Stride Toward Freedom."
Went into his office
one time, by myself.
It was big, though modest.
Had pictures of wife, kids, and him
with that man that went down
in Dallas.
I stayed maybe five minutes.
A great man of this century
worked here at times.
I helped him in my own way.
Looking at his books,
he had sixty-cent biographies of Gandhi,
new, about five of them.
Guess he gave them to friends.

He came from a line
Thoreau
Gandhi
Martin
All men of their times.

JFK and Martin

Two great men stolen from me,
from us, in five years.
I remember,
my birthday 1963.
I didn't get the news
till after sixth period, thank God.
Some teachers got the news after fifth period.
I didn't hang around.
A student ran up to me.
"Did you hear that our President got shot Mr. Duffill?"
Eyes teared, looking up at me
with pain and questioning.
There was no one else I heard in Savannah
say "Our President."
After that I never talked rationally about it.
And my birthday cake stuck in my gut,
and tears came to me for months after,
and still sometimes do come.
A man died last night,
and I didn't know it till this morning.
A man I knew, worked for and even
shook his hand once
He signed one of his books for me.
Lost JFK on Nov. 22, 1963
Lost Martin on April 5, 1968

Sunday April 7, 1968

Went to Spelman College Chapel today,
viewed him lying there immobile,
Remember the fire chat, pulpit roar,
amens echo in the congregation?
In a glass coffin,
had on one of those luxurious,
black suits he sometimes wore,
Mohair I believe,
impeccable dresser.
Confess to tears, holding my son
high in my arms.
We passed men crying,
dark heavy ears,
sad eyes.
Our leader taken.
Tried to steal away his spirit.
It remains however;
we know it will never die.

Hypocrisy

The hypocrisy of the thing is somehow
    maddening;
why it wasn't realized before this
    I don't know—
yet I suppose it was—it's just that
    no action
was taken or really considered
    except
in fleeting moments of restless
    unconcern.
Why we put up with it is
    something
I can't comprehend—
    however
I did, and have, and will (?)
    conform
to the dictates of a raging
    pressure—
BUT I am learning, I am
    stronger
I can now resist, I stand alone.
It does not matter so much,
    results
I worry no longer,
    and
will live such a life
    soon.

Finally moving about
   I
found friends—not always
   agreeing,
but in common we were
   searching
and the answers were
   coming
and the fear was
   abating
and hope was
   arriving.
Books and friends, but more—
   there
were thoughts and thinking,
   a time
to synthesize what was
   learned.
In four years of dished out
   second hand
knowledge, from an institution
   and
(naturally) mass-minded
   education.
But this was more than
   I
had ever had before—
   stifled,
guarded in a home of
   fear

nagging pettiness, jealousies
   but
an intellectual curiosity
   I
adopted.
And a rebellion was
   fomented
which in a quiet-spoken
   way
will continue—and yes—
   is natural.
A home and family of my
   own
gave me a joy and love I can not
   describe.
A security, a relationship of
   Spirit,
a responsibility which was
   fulfilling.
A "citizen" of a community
   emerged
giving a courage, yet
   tameness
and domesticity found its
   way
to the forefront of the
   relationship.
But a Madison Avenue idea
   of

shapeless conformism arose
   and
I tried—God how I
   tried.
And frustrated feelings
   could not
help but flow forward
   in
countless ways—and
   they did.
The classroom—what can I
   say?
For a few moments of inspired
   joy
there are thousands of bland
   bull.
Students long ago initiated to
   ideas
and hatred and prejudices and
   fears
and stupidity, and clichés, and
   generalities
and pigeonholed stereotypes.
   Parents
exhibiting the above traits
   pass
them along—what can I
   DO

but try, hope, inspire and
   try again.
The hatred for anything
   different
prevails over all—or
   fear
would be a better word—
   a defense.
Skin color, religion, politics
   all
come under attack.
   Rationality
seems to have no effect,
   none
whatsoever—oh, for a
   minute
it might (maybe) but the next
   discussion
reveals again the same old
   trifle.
What an injustice is being done
   by
momism and dadism when
   they
don't realize the changing
   world
forcing you to move or be
   cast
aside—("out of the way

you're
holding up traffic").
   Children
suffer later for prejudices
   taught
now—what a disillusion to
   come
later—what a barrier to live
   with.
And I am too and have been
   brainwashed
and am inclined to repeat
   things
I don't really believe—
   absurdities.
I rationalize to understand
   yet
I wonder which is best.
   I
hate to acquiesce in the monstrous
   LIE
but I have done it—why? It was
   easier.
The truth is always hard.
   Truth?
It is all relative from me to
   you—
I'll live mine—you yours
   together

in peace, brotherhood, acceptance
   in
each other and above all,
   love.
Yet the way is open—to
   denounce
and disaffiliate myself—
   alienated
from mass media, pressures,
   distortions
implications—a pure, simple
   dedicated
path to take, weaving through
   skyscrapers
the jungle of obscurity and yet
   recognition,
if not from others then from
   self.
This counts; to exist, perhaps in
   poverty—
yet of the chosen, dedicated
   kind.
Unworried of the entire
   scene
of the American Dream
   bull,
which brings a different type of
   slavery.
To liberate! No more

   chained
to monthly payments, the
   time
clock, the bells regulating
   efficiently
what should never be regulated.
   Guilt
disappears (somehow) regret
   motivates
to places unknown….
and to hell with your bomb,
   god damn
your wars—a curse on
   all
of you who profit on
   exploiting
others—and who gain
   immensely
from hate and fear in
   every way.
Sing the songs on the six-stringed
   instrument
for our bread and for my
   Soul—
this has "freed" me as the
   Proclamation
did the blacks in 1863.
   Emotions
are released as they should be,

   feelings
rip and pour and drain and
   slide
in a dim-lighted room
filled with smoke—listeners and
   non-listeners.
It does not matter; the message
   remains.
Written by others more sensitive
   but
interpreted by me—felt by me
   perhaps
conveyed by me
   Now....
perhaps to someday
   return
perhaps never…who
   knows.
But the choice is made
   the
road less-traveled taken,
   the
weeds as razors
   slice,
carve a life—at least
   honest
     I
       hope....

Find Godliness

Do your thing, find Godliness in whatever way possible,
at all expense, before it is too late.
Eternity does not wait
and time will come too soon for death.
I am dying as I write this now.
I feel death eating me apart.
My pen writes this, not me,
and won't stop moving.
This is more than me on these pages.
I am plugged into the Ground of Being
and though the connection is not the best,
I can hear the words clearly every once in a while.

The Preacher

Met Christ in a laundry mat yesterday
in 14th Street Hippydomb.
They call him "The Preacher."
Making fun of him,
were taunting in their own way.
The Spirit was so strong in him,
I am almost jealous, if it were not love.

Barefoot in the Meadow

I sit barefoot in the meadow;
pasture high above the frozen lake.
The sun is setting over the denuded trees.
It has been a good day.
The shadows are creeping slowly up the hill,
lengthening toward me.
They will reach me soon.
Then it will be time to go home,
home.
A big black and white possum,
his rodent tail high,
just crossed the pasture
some forty yards behind and above me,
never saw me,
I am invisible.

January Horizons

As the sun travels low and moves
around to the right
on January horizons, the moon rises,
white half barrel hooped
skyward above the pines along the opposite shore.
Oh winter Sun, you are love and Spirit,
warming growth buds.
Feeble spirits, my inadequate funds of love and kindness
and honesty and truth—all so inadequate and young.
Teach me your secret in years.
Not now, not ready now for answers.
The ANSWER if there is one, you can't label or pin down.
I am only ready for questions.

My Indian Spirit

I am so much like an Indian
in the December sun,
shirtless, shoeless, reincarnated
Pueblo or Hopi of the before
life, which included a barefoot
south sea island bound pirate too.
When I get my canoe on Lake Louella
we shall know. Then will be the test
of Indian Spirit in residual places
incarnate in my soul.

A Pioneer Wants a Woman

Far from the maddening throng
to the woods where the Spirit
still resides in peace
and where love abounds
from the pot,
and the cup holds sustenance,
for such a mate so inclined,
    a pioneer wants
    a woman sent west.

Summer trips to Maine

In my boyhood childhood the summers were spent gloriously on Great East Lake, in Maine. An old friend of the family whom we so affectionately called "Unkie," almost a father in some ways, at least as far as love and affection were concerned…he owned it with his ill and often ill-tempered mother who really was a suffering angel I see now, for putting up with two boys two years apart for ten summers before she died at eighty something. Thank you dear departed soul, whom we used to have to go say "good morning" to every morning—a hated duty. I can only now fully thank you and love you for your lakeside summer gift. The sun, the clear water, the favorite diving spot, "Redrock," the pier, the tiny row boat, the beach cove around the rocky corner, the big lunch meals out on the porch overlooking the lake one mile wide and eight long. Oh what fantastic boyhood days there which so took the place of the prevalent personal pain of family life. And here I am sitting on a lake in the afternoon mist and breeze, the overcast fog all around, cross-legged on a pier again, a refugee of prevalent personal pain of family life.

December 27, 1967

Meditated on whether to accept offer of full employment in a rock band and am leaning towards NO—for I would have so much less time for the contemplative life up here at the lake. For I would only become deeper involved in ego games. For I would be a group and not just me, thus would be much less free to travel or to split when and if I want to. For I would make too much money, which would be distracting, and I have all that I need now to be comfortable.

No Demands Please

As free as you are now,
no holds held,
no demands please
no rigidified obligations
just a gift given and received
soaking up the feeling
message like a sponge;
absorbing love and
wringing it out
later, over by some dry thirsty
desert plant
in an endeavor to spread
the movement of flowers.
You shook your head
and gave me no words.

The House Fly

Sitting in perspective,
a housefly upon my finger
is held up to the sun
which he obliterates
with his size and
shuts out from my eyes.
He is no different than
the cat I held loving
before the fire yesterday.
He is a housefly yet
part of so much more.
He sits on my finger unafraid,
my hairy face peering up close at him.
He vacuums my guitar callous
with suction mouth,
mine detection apparatus.
He is taking his chances with me.
He could die right now.
Does he know it?
Why does he take this risk?
Is he unafraid?
Does he think similarly about my driving
the expressway every night to work?
Is he that hungry?
Am I?

Do You Know Where I've Been?

Do you know where I've been since this morning, on a long trip; a pilgrimage, very, long…long…a circling the water by land an attempt to connect the circle, to begin in one place and return to it with some kind of knowledge…vision? A pilgrim of snow, ice, wind, swamps, wet bog area hells, with just an occasional sun shining through to stop you, to look up through the fir branches with their tinsel branches telling me today was Christmas for me not Dec. 25. Today.

Why do I write this only for you; for you, no one else but you comes even close to understanding…at least not now and they can never know what I know…indeed what we know at this moment suspended in eternity where we hold hands against the cold for a while. Only a few things…really a lot but simple to say to you and you will understand. Only you know…what I mean.

You are a savior, one of many, yet a tiny minority of the saved among the lost. You were mine. You will be others. You have been a major savior and only the other saved will know the searching, will sense it and be drawn to you for help. Give. Help.

Where? Paths begin around the circle of water, but set them off alone. They have to be alone to reach the top of their mountain, and like you said last night, I didn't know I had been there until I had come down. I have been there, Katie, to the top of my mountain. I didn't know I was so very close to it, I thought it was so far off, but there it was after the hardest struggle to reach it, the sun on the top by a shine which I never can show anyone.

A tree and I said a prayer my eyes closed it was no longer a cold January snowstorm but Spring with the warm April breezes blowing all around and the sun shining down. Then it was over, a brief moment, maybe a lifetime frozen of Being There on the Top. Then it was over and a great fear enveloped me. I clutched at my walking stick. I was on a narrow slick snow ledge about fifty feet directly over the water. I could slip or jump in and be drenched and it really didn't matter but I still felt a tremendous fear. I could go in the water completely come out, go off in the hills, strip off my clothes, lay down and so easily go to sleep, and dream off into Eternity. I had been to the top and that was enough. I wanted to do it so bad. That will be my way to go, when and if I decide to. Socrates was a Man, but Jesus was also.

I went on staggering fear of slipping above the water wanting to return now because I had been to the Top and I can't tell you what is there. I only can say it is there and you have to go alone and words are so inadequate… so inadequate…oh how you know this…I see now…this is so feeble a thing, to put these words down…I apologize to you, and tell you, you will never be loved by anyone else in this way ever again, not like this…

I returned from the Top and Knew that I am Rain, to wash clean. You too are Rain and you know it. We join our single droplets and flow together for a while to join the gathering cloud burst which is coming to cleanse the lost. I will never curse the rains again. Let them come. I know everything is getting clean. I see the droplets; in fact I search them out on cold January hikes in the snow.

When You Are Gone

We will
    miss you when
        you are gone,
but
you will still
    be here anyway.
    A part
    of your beauty
    remains always.

—*TWD*

I Know Why

I know why I had that bursting mystical period of creativity on the bay in the sun in Montrose by the cliffs one week before I had made one of the biggest emotional and important decisions of my lifetime. I gave up the last thread, before the first marriage cord, which broke two months later. I gave up at last, after going to three post graduate Colleges and Universities in a Masters Degree attempts. At beautiful black Atlanta University, I knew I could take it no longer; nor did I want the Degree at all; nor did I want to teach safely installed in a college professorship role. I wanted to live! I wanted to BE… BE… and be free to follow my madness, my vision.

I want to:

gaze for hours at the sun.

listen to the crows cackle in the distance.

hear the roar of the waters spilling out of the lake down the flood

gate.

see the sparrows eat morning bread crumbs thrown out the night

before into the snow.

see the moon on the ice white road so bright as we walk.

see the deep blue sky top covering ocean depths under her white

waves.

Georgia

I love Georgia
love her immensely.
Traveling her shores
from her mountains
to the sea
her depth secret.
I love Georgia
so much.
And especially Atlanta
her bustling center
the midriff of the state
the powerful metro source
the guider and manipulator
of the body.
A thousand nerve wires
stretched on concrete
leading in from the north
following out to the south
still moving traffic
expressways to Atlanta
the source
lying the strength.
Of my love
Georgia
your pine crested beauty
and wrinkle faced farms
frightened cold faced executives
driving home in tin cubicles all alone.

What does it mean?
What can I say?
Love to you
God bless you.
Just north of Atlanta
in the woods of Georgia
her piney stems, green resources
of a proud people, a proven area,
sometimes rebellious
in these southern regions,
I stand in the south with her.
Independent
in her public forest
which she holds back from
public domain,
from federal tampering
I'll stay living with
Georgia.
   Living close to
Georgia,
   living in
Georgia,
always withdrawing
slowly and gently from her
if I have to travel elsewhere.
Who needs to go?
It's all here.
Her ears blush.

Savannah squirms,
and Augusta gathers
closer to hear better.
No one loves like the poet
or the one who loves God
who is really turned on.
We turned on to Georgia,
turn on to her beauty
her magic in shining
sparkling eyes I see nightly
not in dreams, but real
above watching the winter
moon widen, thicken,
showing her pregnancy to me
personally,
raising garments,
I see her full blown
at the end of the month.
High round and white
I watch her descend in the sky.
Glide through her life
giving a light
to call poets and lovers
in March darkness.
Trees whistling to
a symphony of wind,
different notes telling me
I love Georgia,
my mistress.

And so your highways,
long pearly thighs
leading to Atlanta
expressways,
to the city center
following you south,
when it's necessary,
when I need to
feel the need fully
to go to Atlanta.

Savannah

Down in Savannah
the beach rolls in on the tide
daily, twice revealing crabs
(not those kind)
on the sand
and shells and
my footprints
barefoot stretching out before me.
The horizon sun set,
ocean fire burning
in August, near
Tybee lighthouse,
a beacon for the lost,
pointing toward heaven.

Hilton Head Island

But I could make love to
Georgia on South Carolina
beaches at sunset,
dripping salt and brine
from sea dips into
her beauty
and fall past heavenly gates
to a climatic and lovely
ending.

Small Town Georgia

On the small town
south Georgia streets,
a young man
wearing a pickup truck,
driving a short haircut,
does an obscene gesture
at me with that
dirty middle finger nail,
a move learned in school
where they don't like
long hair.
Even if George Washington,
and Custer's last stand,
and Lincoln's beard,
and tough warrior Indians,
had it long;
even the carpenter from Nazareth,
who I love
for his love and strength and godliness,
had long hair and a beard.
Why didn't they put his picture
on the billboard on 14th street
saying "Beautify America, get a haircut"?
Someone is afraid.

In the Warmth of Her Arms

I bring little pine trees
back from my woody walks
and plant them along the
raw red dirt gash
on the hill by the cabin
to hold the dirt.
How can you hold the dirt
from sliding down hill
after the earth is cut
and left exposed?
Why do those that shovel
not know?
Dirt and shit grow
the loveliest of flowers
to place in a wreath
for the holy head of
Georgia,
around her golden hair
hanging long
past her shoulders.
She plays a recorder
from late sun meadows,
her tune so gentle,
calling me,
seducing me to
forget my words
my paper,

my don't know if it fits
poem or whatnot
and come to her
my Georgia
to her arms to lay softly
buried in the warmth of her love.

Fall

Lying again among the fallen leaves
brown and twisted, gnarled hands uplifted
too late, February blanketed of indifference
brown twisted souls once green and young
yes tender, oh living, oh growing
wow performing.
What happened?
To find you here around
my life, reminding me of fall,
and death, and time,
      reorganizes itself for me
      to give me time
      to do something
      besides
      gaze at the dead.
The dead
lie dead,
leave them die,
please.

Who Writes These Words?

It is the Spirit that is not me,
that writes these words. It is you too.
I deny my words, negate responsibility for them
and blame them on creeping holy madness
which whispers,
"I've never been Saner in my life."
Where I must have copped out on my mission
and sent in this form, this shell to America
to be tested, stereotyped, branded.
India would have been so much easier.
Yet the test is here, now.
I am losing my mind, losing my mind
and gaining one much bigger.
It is frightening…

Feb. 3, 1968

I just know that I have an awful long way to go, much of it alone, most of it probably. The world must be left to go by itself for a while… without me. Think you can make it world? Methinks you have made it long without me and never really noticed. In fact you could make do without a lot of us and wouldn't miss us, not a bit. Maybe I'll come back and maybe I won't. It is much the same and makes little difference to you.

Feb. 12, 1968

Sometimes, when you are afraid, it is hard not to look back down the path you've been for security. It is always true that doubt is there no matter which path you take. "Should I have taken the other one?" Do not doubt the path you are on—be strong and not afraid. You are on the correct trail though the signs are more difficult to decipher.

    Thank you,
        Lord for her strength
        when I so needed it.

Poems

My Son

And you ask: "What is time, what is space?"
    I think and ponder—stare into your face
most intently, grope for an answer in the dark.
    "Time is the seasons and space is the race
that we all must staggeringly start
    and sadly finish, knowing all the while
that the hour is relative and man-made;
    that the present will be past (like the flickering smile
on your lips which soon shall fade);
    this is not the answer that the scientist
will give, nor the statement for the
    life you must live.
Live it completely and know in your heart
    that we put you here, your race to start,
and time is the only boundary that wills to confine
    you; as here I stay and on you go—son of mine.

TWD, 10-24-64

The Quest

My mind open wide to the light that would shine
   only it's not here for me;
here and where and I wonder where
   the eyes to help me see;
at last I surmise to my surprise
   that I am totally free
to decide not what is best for the rest
   but what is best for me.

Alone I am with self, on a path
   through damp dark forest
with a light to the right and in the haze
   of the maze of my quest;
my eyes will blur to it and I look to see
   if anyone, besides me, and lo:
they are there, but it is curious though
   for they all wield a protective shield.
And at last I understand that I will die a man
   surrounded but yet alone to the throne
if it is, and—if I can.

TWD, 12-26-64

November 22, 1963

The smile disappears
   a tear
unevaporated
       unincorporated
alone unlicensed alienated
   drips rolls falls
      flips
on caricature faceless image
    of hurt pain
    and
then to cry stare ahead
       seeing nothing nothing.
Why?
   JFK is dead.

TWD, 3-1965

My Peace Cabin *Feb. 11, 1967*

Rocked-ridged ledged
    of ruination of
        my fantasies—escape
   dream cabin nestled
   deep in pine-Georgia
     hill which was
        discovered in love
    and beauty
high above the clear
        stream creek
sitting on silver rail
    rocked foundation—
      the rest
          has burned…
all the physical and
material
          shall burn and
perish while
          fantasies
dream clings like fresh
    green moss
        to a cemented
foundation which
    in
times of hopefulness
    we try to call life…

I Thought

I thought it
        was a jeweled
rock 'n
      I peed upon it
'n it was only
        an old
rusted-worn
          tired
              beer can.
What can
      it all
          MEAN?????????????

TWD, 6-25-66

Like A Brain Bubble

Like a brain bubble perched perilously
   on undulating sea
                    of life
I float unattached to the others;
and I've seen you
     try to break it, at least shake it
       reform it
           into
     God knows what
        other shape.
Maybe just another
              wave
                  to lap gently
in tune with the others—
                concordant
would be easier than being a bubble
            which is only a
short termed irregularity
        unsymmetrical
in the symmetry which others
        call
          life.
With words
      looks
          attitudes
              actions
we flail attempting a puncture of the
froth-vision of our seas to drown in

                    the ego
                        of
                    personality
                    differences.
And I do it
                so do you—and just because
I don't weep in the night is no sign I don't
                grieve—to see
something between us perish
                as water evaporates slowly
to the atmosphere
                only to return
                        again…elsewhere…
Is our love
                drying—evaporating
from puddles of orgasmic shimmers of
sun soaked sensations?
                Was
it only that—do we fool ourselves?
                Will
we find out before our bubbles bump brashly
and we two
                crumble crash—both absorbed
in waters of humanity
                        never to see each
other as a trembling dream again—
        only indistinguishable waves on the shoreline
of eternity…

TWD, 3-7-67

Winter's Come Early

I have done many things and been many
    all in one
I have strode my 26 years as the
    tiny green
garden snake so struggles
    silently
on his belly down dewey-wet
    spring paths
knowing he still has a summer
    and a fall
before winters chilly finality
    brings him
to his knees to seek refuge
    at last;
and knowing it may end ANY
    moment
with but a pussycat's pounce
    or possibly
a well-intentioned club wielded
    by a
PTA mother who kills ALL legless
    sliding things—
who judges all such reptiles from
    rattlesnake
standards with Freudian
    reference to
        Adam,

and hit hard as bones and skin
   crumble quickly
while frail north winds blow
   cool—"Perhaps
Winter's coming early this
   time."

TWD, 6-21-66

You Too

And you too
         my friend
will face death
   and know
the days of joy you
      have thus
         denied me.

TWD, 5-4-67

Foster Father

Bastard child of freedom
    whom nobody really
claims at the checkout
    counter,
        why do you
cry so constantly—
    collectively
        in
the human channel
    of consciousness?
No one will adopt you
    from your orphaned
ugliness of forced
        isolation;
their nursemaid
    restive
responsibility will refuse
    you
        rationalizing voyeur
vulgarisms
    of security…
Your nightmare wail will
    echo frustration
        down institutional
clichés piously proclaiming
        you;

your piss-stained bed
    sheets will stay
unchanged—they're afraid
    to come near
        to
    reality's discomfort;
your laughter in nightlong
    hall corridors
will clang empty from
    barred windows
        of wishfulness
to keep your body
    chained
        with only
your name floating
    meaningless
        on parental parole.
But I saw your
    little angel face mirrored
from my depth—a glimpse
    of your challenge calling
        me to unlock
        the gate
            of an
                Orphan's Odyssey
and dare—or attempt to be
    a foster
        father of
            Freedom…

TWD, 2-15-67

Dying Embers

Midnite mother,
        thoughts bubbling
in the cauldron of your nakedness
        burning embers
        from your soul
which no clothes dare envelop…
cloud cloth drip drop
                cleanse
cool passioned pain
                of closeted chambers
rain in darkness
          slowly sizzle
burning coals sliding rivulets
    of life-blood
    down drains of adjustment…
    leaving lives of quiet desperation—
   cold coal on the warmth
              of the earth…

TWD, 2-21-67

Brown Eyes

Questioning sensitive eyes
        surely I don't
        begrudge your sincerity;
your pained flickering lids
        like fireflies flickering
        in my frosted forest…
tell me the revolution is
        not lost yet…
        shed some silence
to trickle tremulously
    on
        Cavalry's
                cheeks…

TWD, 2-21-67

Plotting Pete's Peace

A plot of acreage
                some 37 of those
                arbitrary divisions
near Stone Mountain, Georgia
                have turned me on
                      recently
as I have explored beyond—
            beyond
the dazzling outer countenance
to the dark moss covered rolling rock
                tree lined
                    flower moist brook.
Like a beautiful woman
   the deepest sensitive joy
   lies hidden
       hidden and cover clothed
   waiting
   waiting for the esthetic
   hiker to probe lightly…
      find…
         and
           fully appreciate.
No one had been to this spot
    in a long while—maybe
    never before—
virginity or non-virginity
   that is NOT the question

      in most cases;
the result in this beauty was
    the same
           clean
unpolluted flowing waters of life,
no trash, chewing gum wrappers
        beer bottles—
if someone had seen this,
    conquered and loved it
    in body and spirit
    I have a bond with him,
    a common appreciation
    of loving essence
       and that he
told no one apparently
    of the round rising rocks,
    moss covered
    to make the hand
    more
        softly
            caressing.

TWD, 4-8-67

Poetic Bliss at Fishin' Lake

Poetry, like Seurat's bather with
              spin-casting outfits,
is the worm on the hook of reality
open
     and
exposed
for all to nibble at the bait—
    infrequently
swallowing it
           but picking
                 only—
                only
rarely are fish caught.
    When
they are,
       inevitably they realize
their sex was a guise for the
institutionalized hook which
not only has killed your worm
        but
           bittered
your fillet in guileful
                  betrayal.

TWD, 3-20-67

Crab

Torn picked at until
    the inner pureness
(which I know is there)
    begins to fade and
slide across the beachhead
    of the mind as claws
drag slowly destroying by
    friction that which it
wanted to possess and hold.

Tasty morsel of love
    your crab has held you
too tight and has
    invariably crushed you
the life blood of love
    flowing crimson red in
rivulets down the sandy
    beach to join the oceans
        massive
heartbreaking sadness…

TWD, 3-29-65

Being Free

…"Wait a while longer
        you'll see
                that being free
is an internal state
        of the mind,
           a rare kind
of person that is
        independent of spirit,
           unhindered by the grip
of opinion's whip which flays to conformity
                and ultimate uniformity.
Can one give it, deny it,
        or touch it—just try it;
            ask the prisoner
ask the child or the warden
            the slave yet unpardoned
      the native wild
see what they say
        try to explain it away
           with words interplayed."
…"An internal state
        of the mind you say
           " Are you sure?",
said the student of time
        who off time climbed
           to ring the chime

```
to line them up
        in good form
                each with a numbered form
still almost warm
                    from the robot machined
        which can only mean
we are all equal
                to the IBM man
                            who will try if he can
to give to you
            and then to me
                        his own special brand
pumped out of a can
                stuffed full of sand
                        FREE-DUMB
                    Are
                        you
                                ready??
```

TWD 3-12-66

Darkness

Darkness descends
    quaking
night-time sounds
    foaming
to the ears enunciate
    ringing
roar of inconsistencies
    making
that a reality
    noting
only that relativity prevails
    warning
to frighten the insane
            to
                sanity.
Quirks of nature smirk
    obscenities
croak fitful froth platitudes
    absurdities
ring from brow-beaten
    unentities
cry out all judgement false
    chickidees
for only the dead
          listen
            to
              you.

TWD, 1-5-66

A Busy Signal

Like a phone, an instrument
    only,
        acted upon
    hung-dialed
        hung up
in its limitations
    I
am connected
        to your world
by a twisted cord of umbilicus,
a phallic wired
    stimulus-response
           pole,
and a
    faulty
        mouthpiece.

TWD, 3-20-67

Driving Wheel *April 20, 1967*

Convictions—
    like the wheel of steering
inertly guide
  without fire
      in the engine of action.

Sun Setting

(I)

The sun setting
    on the Bay,
        miles of upward
            outward
            expansion.
From the cliff height
from my head sight
up and out
a firey tower
a whirling dervish
sending golden fire pebbles
out into the water
to extinguish sizzlingly.
My love,
it is somehow my beacon,
a light
calling us to a magical world
with a mighty wand wave
from the Sun
to the Sons.

(II)

Like a big heavy round
molten lead ball
falling
in slow motion
into the sea.

Some kind of an hour glass
giving us time units
as our measure.
A giant crimson Christmas
tree ball from
the Omnipotent-
He dangles it in a
November tease,
I reach for it with
words
seeing it smoldering
sink into horizoned waters.

(III)

And there it goes
a scarlet crown
bowing at last,
quickly now,
submerging the
scalding bald
vermilion pate
from view.
    Sun Set.
What are you??
Like a friend
again in temporary farewell;
a lovers fading
hot embrace
till tomorrow morning,

while
a grayness pallor
fills the cheek of the loverless
and we
sink into a wintry
underworld of darkness
until the fireball shall
rise in the morn.

(IV)

Only a titian tangerine
sallowness remains
now,
hinged on the horizon
suspended over the water
like a giant halo
encircling this part
of the sphere.
And I wonder
at the marvel
      miracle
      mystery,
loving to be in awe,
digging for no one answer,
      for no rebuttal,
just a wandering
      wondering
      whaler,

a seafarer perched
on a cliff above the
briny water,
the sun soul probing
with a glistening golden harpoon
across the
bay—brandishing
my brain
in brilliance
stirring my soul to behold.

TWD, Oct. 26, 1967, Mobile Bay

JON-I-THIN, in Albany Jail

Jon-i-thin, they have caged your body
    and your soul tells me why;
for it flies with the winds
    emitting faint love-cries,
and it lights upon the rooftops
    and envelops the streets below—
"all men are free and brothers"
    and you're in jail—for it is so.
Yes the roaches share your bread
    and rats dance across the floor.
A wooden bench must be a bed
    and iron bars an ungiving door.
And though they try to take your pride
    and deny that you exist,
you only love with a heart-opened grid
    a blade of grass through
            the morning mist.

Born Free

"Born free" echoes the eagle
sang clear in the morn and
whispered the word to my ear;
and I knew not how nor why
and nor will I fear
the weight of choice-demands,
you must decide on plans
and carry forth—
        yes act!
now ain't
    that a fact....

TWD, June 25, 1966, Clarks Creek

Why???

Men seem more determined to
    flay at inconsequentials
than to come to grips with
    simplicity—necessity
as the core of life is
        sweet.

Why have wise men walked
    out of their palaces
to sleep sound on a pallet
of pine boughs
in the wilderness?

Why did sweet Jesus
go forty days in the
    bleak mountain
and return with forgiveness
    and love—but
not to his carpenter tools?

Why did Buddha leave it
    all for a simple
life of poverty? And what
    about Tolstoy—and
Thoreau at Walden, and
    Gandhi facing
an assassin's bullet with

    all he owned
upon his back or able to be
    carried in his hands??

America, when will you
    wash y'r linen
in the clear streams 'stead
    of in greasy 'lectric
        laundra-machines??

Who Are You?

    I'm
Jesus Christ 'n only thinking
   of forgiving all y'r sins.

    I'm
Douglas McArthur feeling
   the Philippines c'n
sink in oceanic hell
   'fore I'll return.

    I'm
Profumo thinking Christine
   Keeler Venus Joy Mound
    was worth it all.

    I'm
Mae West feeling in m'
   heart all the men who
wished t' feel it in m' breast.

    I'm
Henry David Thoreau who
   wishes his Mexican
killerwartaxes were
   never paid.

    I'm
Gaugan in South Seas
   wishing his syphlitic soul

had never been laid.
    I'm
junkie Burroughs knowing
    he never should've
stuck a veined tube
    in blue rivers 'f blood.

    I'm
Bob Zimmerman who
    desires t' be Dylan
'n can't, but who digs
    singing soul in cantos.

    I'm
Vincent Van Gogh fallen
    heavy, one-eared
upon the ground leaving
    the gun 'n palette t'
        drift lazily down
            thru the ages…

    I'm
Lester Maddox peddling
    only white drumsticks
from a basket o' fear.

    I'm
Martin Luther King trying
    t' tell 'em o' love
'n nonviolence, 'n only
    reaching t' one ear.

I'm
Moses who fell on his
   face in the desert
while the children of
   Israel walked on.

I'm
Joseph who did put
   it t' MarySweetSoul
n' matter what they keep
   telling ya.

I'm
Lenin in London Library
   plotting paper-back
     revolutions.

I'm
Leary from Harvard whom
   LSD doesn't turn on
           any more.

I'm
y'r brightfaced virgin
   mother who desires
the male phallus but
   continues t' pray it
away while the
     aching remains.

I'm
y'r frustrated father
    who wanted t' lay
all the pretty girls
    but who was
chained t' contracts 'n
    outmoded morals.

I'm
you who feel lonely
    pain 'n fear all
too often 'n whose heights
    of happiness
erupt not often nor
    high enough.

TWD, July 4, 1966

Denial

Warm sun nature's god,
      so
much has been denied
      me,
has been denied by
      me,
really how much
      longer
can I do this to myself,
      rejecting
the deeply felt instincts
      of
my being, of my
      Soul?

TWD, March 29, 1965

So It Must Be

Demands expectations hurl
    at an absent minded
brain grow dreary—bored
    living in a vacuum
of nothingness.
The more required
    less given—it.
Has to come
            must come
sincerely and naturally.
    Pure love for what one
is, begets likewise.
    Selfish demanding love
begets bitter antipathy.
    So it is
            so it must be.

TWD, March 29, 1965

The Decision
Seeming to be
    many in one,
the mind vacillates,
    sidestepping
what is basic.
    Intangling
as the perennial
    spider, in
details, petty
    decisions…
only that this time
    the spider
himself has been
    webbed;
"fate" has caught
    hold…
what decision is left?

Days

Day oh day of
   endless
days rolling in
   monotonous
agony seeming
    never
to end in a crashing
   climax
but brandishing the
   ever present
ax of boredom which
   never clearly
slices but weighs
   heavily
pressing dumbly on the
   mind's eye
or brain or mass of
   cranium
        flesh
or whatever it is that
   gives
life to head-located
   cells
enabling thought-like
   spirits
        to spiral-madness…

Cyclical Patterns

Wing whispered chant
   from file cabinet trees
growing from cloud linings
    mystically floating high
       tripping daintily
from department store
   elevator shafts
where mince meat
   mice droppings
greet the day
        in decomposing
wonderment
        'n stare back
with a twinkle on the bridged nose
       of
   cyclical patterns.
Wandering monks in motorcycle
  helmets
       clash with
feminine vacuum cleaners
  for bargain basement
    toylots
      'n sandpiles
to take home to their
        pet lemming
        who leach
        breast-mouthed
        to cyclical patterns.
Fountain eyed sales jingoes

    smile leeringly
    frost gathered
      tooth
to each other while noon time
    white skinned
        suits
    drink mashed
       potatoes
   in saddened
   cyclical patterns.
Mortared mountains erupt jack hammering
   vibrations in
   non-stillness
      of the daytime
               nightmare
n' crouch featherfooted
   fingering latch springs
      ejaculating upward
        in
        cyclical patterns.
Rug grimmed rapers ring cash registers
    announcing King Leopold
'n his 18 Mucous Membranes
who perform on dancing elbows
   for languid thighed
     ceramic countenances
    continuing
    cyclical
        patterns.

TWD, 7-29-66

What is Left to Believe in?

The feeling is with me
    and it will not leave.
It pains, it nags
    it pulls and tears—
not much left to believe
    in now—at least
as far as the value
    extends from society
to the individual I am
    or hope to be.
To realize at last,
    all is a farce
requires a courage fast
    from within (where?)
I have to face alone
    the future
to attempt to know
    the animal, angel,
madman, artist
    believer, skeptic
or whatever else
    there is.
I never meant to hurt,
    hinder, cause
pain—it just seems
    to come out
that way—to blurt
    explain, in a
stumbling, bumbling
    rumbling jargon

only resembling slight
   communication
of any sort.
And yet change
   can not be
forced on me
   from another
much less from
   myself.
Spiraling downward
mind slowly growing
   imbalanced
from it all
        twisted moving
beyond reality—sphere
   spiraling
only downward away
   from
        here
to the journey's end of
   madness.
Angelic—insanity open
   your hairy spider
octopus arms, envelop
   this
poor soul and give him
   peace
and unstable stability
   locked
        forever…

TWD, March 29, 1965

My Old Friends

A premature withering
of the juices of life;
my old friends,
upon seeing them again,
are edgeless somehow—
seemingly afraid of
new experiences,
set in a comfortable niche
they are mostly silent
        dead-eyed
         waiting…
         for what??
My old compatriots
   back then
   I was wintry;
   frozen…
   afraid
   to be alive
   to be self-fulfilled.
Being spring now
   I bid to hold your
   senses in my palms
   while the essence trickles
   slowly through
   enlaced fingertips
   sparkling in the moonlight;
And I'll write ambitious poems
   in an effort,

    for you to read
    tucked within your covers
    late at night,
    while I walk the darkness
    in scarce disguise.
My loved ones,
    here is an illusion
    a fleeting mirage
    in the desert
    calling you in an echo
    to live
    before it is too late—
    To love
    not to wait
    for timeless futures;
And while you smile at
    my thought beams
    smug in your bedding
    wrapped in sheets
        of security
    I will be busy
        baptizing
          the self
            in the sandlot
              of my blue mirage.
My old cohorts—
      desert flowers bloom
      and will not wait to be
      appreciated;
be cognizant of your color

        your fragrance
           your beautiful
                brevity—
envelop
turn on to yourself
dig fully
the mirror
of the puppet self
in exaltation
upon the stage
of life—
Be a whirling dervish
    with hummingbird senses
      hovering
      listening
      feeling,
              your toes
    spinning the world in
    twirls—
    dance with me until they
    drag us off the stage
    with a butterfly net.
Smiling at it all
laughing at ironies
loving the mysteries
when placed in the arms
of white frocked morticians—
greet them as an immigrant
having few wayfaring regrets.

Blackness

"Color conscious" she
    spoke,
a warm smile on a
    brown
creamy face. To look for a
    Negro
in a sea of white faces
    standing
out like a black kat
    from
a flood of white dogs
    panting
heat-like for the loose
    un-hung
up feeling which can't
    come.

I Was There

Where the sun rose deftly
        in the trees
in the swamp hollowed
       blanket of Eden
caressing a mire of tangled muck
    too complex
to ever figure out
      (oh yes!
  I was there…)
Where the desert sands
        burned palate
punishing thinly and roasting evenly
  the remaining brain cells
and extended near-corpse
        counting
grains…too complex
      too much
(oh yes!
    I was there…)
Where the wine was sweet
       and soft
delight dangling from
      the bottle
numbing eventually
     the brain
whence came

           the awareness of it all
you try to escape
              —there is none
(oh yes!
       I was there)
Where the face turns grimly
                    again
to the north and the
                  iron tracks
fold fondly clinging
              to the sphere
and false hope melts daintily
                as the snow
between the ties
           at the breakout of Spring
(oh yes!
       I was there)
Where marchers turned
           the corner
flailing determined bodies
             to the capital
in a sea of black and white
             to different
directions—but interior job of justice
    will be finished
            (oh yes!
                  I was there…)

Where the Klansman
                    rode a car of
cowardice
            balancing the jaugernought
careening
            alongside to fire shots
of doom from the gloom
                        of one
to the light of another
                    heart
prejudiced—blind hatred
                    lurking under
the surface of us all
                    (oh yes!
                            I was there)
Where the alienated
                    trod the dim-lit
corridors
            of the street and mind—
mindful of the glossy
                    crowd
                            covering
the periphery of the eye
                    on all sides
        surrounded
            yet
            alone

                    (oh yes!
                                I was there)
Where the jaded Jew
                jackknifed his body
to the crevice
            of the gentile's heart
and attic
        in defiance and fear
of Nazi
        Hitler-like madness
which didn't die
            in the bunker—in May '45
        (oh yes!
                I was there)
Where the gentiles met
                and touched
and quivered in
        ecstasy
                and drew apart
only for a moment
            —delicious sweet
time of rebirth
            of spirit
                    and
                            body.
        (oh yes!
                I was there)

Where the vertical iron
                          bars of
emotional defeat
              held the
                        inmate
from the madness
                  locked outside
insane asylum
          interior
                  to cling
to psychotic
          womb of the mind.
          (oh yes!
                  I was there)

Monday *Nov. 1976*

We both want to help,
    we both hinder
      hassle city.
How do we escape from
        our minds?
How do we find
          the love we need,
           the love we have to have?
Or do we
        (cynically)
           give up the ghost
              on everything?
I fall on the field of battle
        screaming—NO!
    Might go down
        but won't quit.
    The spectators
          may be yelling
          "go fool"
                "get it anyway."
        I say
          "but what?"

Decency

"Like they can't ignore
> 20 million

people—though they tried
> like

hell for so long." Nobody
> gives

anybody anything it seems,
> even

decency comes hard
> pressed.

A Role

I am a role—
> a role in a

toilet paper play
> torn

apart
> from time
>> to time

and
> used
>> accordingly…

TWD, 3-12-67

Interstate 85

Never signaling to change
    lanes, shifting side shafts
piercingly entering my domain
    without warning
    to encroach on my
pumpkin plan which
    so perilously perches
on the pinnacle of
    preservation.
Shift gears—speed up—
    slow down—go in
reverse through the back streets of town
down alleys of adversaries
    who creep noiselessly
never sounding their
    horn before locking
bumpers in trashcan
    channel of TV temper.
Whose bird was that in
    my nest last week
flashing public downy
    feathers of fortune
and misfortune as I
    wound through curving
cubicles on the back road
    of life with no
    roadmap to
fly home fortune's fellah.

TWD, 1-29-67

Three Chains

Three chains, 'n the one
      in the middle
it's plain for anyone
      to see,
is trapped by the other
      'n must always be
the most unfree—pulled
      'n pushed many ways
until that day he enters
      the fray
          of life,
claiming triangles
      are a drag, 'n
breaking free of that bag
      becomes one of
          two
'n thus all that's
      left is me 'n you…

TWD, 7-8-66

Songs

Underdose of Faith

Got a reeling in my head, got a shaking in my soul
There's a feeling can't be said, can I tell what can't
    be told
It's been such a long time, for love to come around
Been such a long trip, to end up on this side of town

Chorus
Throw away your excuses, why do you wait
And the fool
And the fool
Knows an underdose of faith

Yes I've been this way before, there's a road sign
    in my mind
Past the warning light ahead, just before the detour sign
The avenues and expressways, float beyond the reach
    of time
The alley and the driveways, feel the creeping force
    of my mind

It's been such a long time, to the garden sense of rhyme
It's been such a long trip, to the Eden glow of time
From the dead you're on the rise only the living please
    come around
She holds the gate for the wise, she denied your burial
    ground

Written on Jan.10, 1968

Gypsy Woman

Chorus
She's a gypsy woman
She's a new kind of woman
Ain't got a hang-up to worry about

In her covered wagon cycle she moves
    about on her own terms
She gives freely with feeling her gift
    that eternally burns
The brothers run to greet her, they know she comes
    astride the cycle stallion you see
She does nothing but yearn

She pays no taxes on her anarchist yield
She plants fully in the springtime of her fertile field
And the rains of time tell us the fruit is real
You gather in the harvest or what's left that
        the starving didn't steal

Written in February 1968

North Woods Holdout

Wind goes round my cabin
Snow drifts cluster upon the ground
Sit so safe in my north woods holdout
And I never left your town   *(repeat)*

I've a book for every occasion
There's a friend to meet every need
Once, twice I blend with the seasons
It's all one when your soul's been freed   *(repeat)*

The world's all sham and illusion
Smoke dreams cloud over my head (bed)
My loved one we unite in a fusion
And I never left your bed (head)   *(repeat)*

The child he's father of manhood
So many dreams are left behind
Grow tight, do right, they tell you
But listen to your dreams, they're divine   *(repeat)*

Written November 1968

Free Man Child

Ideas wrapped in swaddling clothes
In my manger mind I search in those
Not forsaking the sun that unlocks the freeze
See the humble child upon his knees

Chorus
Running, running, running, running
Running free
Free man child

In the mountains crouched a monk in black
With his rice bowl tied upon his back
Who said the silence with a lip search smack
Closed peace eyes inward to his mind train track

The ocean crashed sealing my find
With an ego blast that crumbled my mind
That had separated me from the sign
That points to the path of our pilgrims in kind

What's a guru, what's a teacher,
What's a prophet got to say to you
Would you listen children
Or would you just say how do you do

We been strangers in a strange land
Searching for a way to get out
Tell me Siddhartha what's the secret
Your soul is about

The chief flew the cookoo and a man
Gave his life for his friend
Do you believe gentle souls, we can
Whip the big nurse in the end

Written in February 1968

Tam at the Bottom of the Barrel in 1968.

There's a Way

Chorus
When the words sometimes slip away
And there's really nothing left to say
Please look at me, try to see
There's a way, there's a way

If I opened up like a card hand upon your table
And let you know just where I stand
Would you think any different
In the image of your reflected man

Is the mirror still held so tightly
Or is it broken down upon the floor
What is it that you so painfully ask
I hear an echo, what more, what more?

As I lay sleepless far into the night
And wonder which way to turn
I perceive the task but no light
So in lighting my candle I'll continually burn

Written December 1968

What Kind of Lover

I dreamed of some kind of angel
Just like a fool
A mistake in the mind of a misfit
Like the type you made back in school

Chorus
What kind of lover do you think you are
Have you opened your heart to catch a falling star

You play the twist with words and phrases
And thought beams clash in the dark
It began with play games of passion
And it ends on a bench in the park

Do you cry when a cloud goes crashing
Do you curse your concrete fate
Have you ever crouched alone in a closet
And weeped for a woman that won't wait

Written December 1968

Twenty Six Miles to Mobile

Twenty six miles to Mobile
Got to move on down the line
Twenty six miles to Mobile
Got to move on down the line
To see you, to see you, to see you
Be so fine

Traveling on the Gulf Coast
I see you traveling there
Traveling on by the Gulf Coast
I see you traveling there
To see you, to see you, to see you
Be so fair

Baldwin County to Mobile, it's not too far to go
To see you, to see you, to see you
Be the one

Fairhope to Mobile, not too long to go
To see you, to see you, to see you
Be the one

Mobile to Atlanta, a lot farther to go
To see you, to see you, to see you
Be the one

Chorus
Mobile seems like a long way babe
When you're walking in the rain
I got busted down in Birmingham
Ain't got no money for no train

Your body's known a thousand hands
But that don't make no mind
Just know that when I see you
It's gonna be so fine

Written Spring 1969

Half-Satisfied

Chorus
I've always been a rebel, half-satisfied
Look one way and go up the other side
Why wait for me, why wait for you
I keep going and going through

Through the mountains and valleys wide
Trying not to laugh and not to cry
I was raised one way and my mind says why
I had to turn out on the other side

But I dig the edge from where I live
It's not too flat it's more like a shiv
Like a dagger you know it's got a point
Come on mama light up that joint

Written October, 1975

Ask Me Why

Yes, being in love can make you smug
Sweep all those problems under the rug
But that just tends to build up after a while
I'll take your tears and a smile

Smile at the love and hate in the aisle
Can those feet become a mile
Who knows who can say the way
Hate can be love or might can be may

Chorus
It's a weird world when you come from left field
When one bite can become a meal
Oh being in love can make you smug
Sweep your problems under the rug

What the hell you say from home plate
Can a mistress become a mate
Can I grab a piece of the sky
How can anyone ask me why

Written August, 1979

City Hermit

Chorus
It's a prison the city hermit claimed
I know what I want and have dead aim
If I don't get it—it's bad news for me
From what you have—it's hard to flee

Eating in regular restaurants to have contact
With cooks and waitresses who probably don't
    give a damn
But who am I to say or cast blame
On a lonely mind who has to have an aim

Meeting many people who want no long term contact
I don't want marriage or some kind of contract
Just commitment to each other
Or friends, lovers or brothers

Finally you meet what you like to have
"Almost too much" he screamed aloud
And it's true he's said a prayer
For what comes down in the world out there

Written Aug., 1979

A Human Place

Have you ever loved a woman
So much you tremble in pain
Love can be a drag—hard to
Let you sleep in the rain

The rain, the sun—makes no difference
For any future loves I need no reference *(repeat)*
Just the satisfied look on your face
Our love has given me a human place

Chorus
Give me a human place my dear
No animal hunting round
Give me a human place my dear
And I will love you down into the ground

Written Nov., 1979

The Best Thing

It's so hard laying next to you my dear
You know I want to wake you and hold you near
But you work the late shift and need that rest
So I love you and let you sleep and that be the best

Chorus
It's the best thing for the best one
I want to see you looking good and feel alright
It's the best thing for the only one
So much trust and love it is our might

Hard to separate the might from the right
I want to love you hold you close all night
I'm just a sometime musician with a few gigs
I heard people dig our rig

Dig our rig—it don't go up or down
Since we met it has eclipsed this town
Hanging round the country and in the lake
You know it's the best that I can make

Written Nov., 1979

Bottom Blues

Many have touched me
But none have held me as you have
If you think you ain't a savior look again
This is one man you have saved

So many years to get to this place
It all before seemed as if it was a race
Get and grab and run up the wall
If we ain't together I hit bottom—no case
The bottom blues

Chorus
We've all had the bottom blues
Trying to follow society's rules
But you can follow your dream
I know true love is our tool
I'm positive I can change my way
It's barely there and if I will I may
Hold you tightly together always
You know that is our way

Written March, 1980

Lonely Place

To try to feel independent again is a bitch
So hung up on you—can I be your perfect brand
Sometime there's a doubt and hurt all around
So if it ends I'll be so messed up down town

Down town alleys and sleazy back room joints
Peace of mind in a dozen weird churches
I meditate on mistakes of mine
And how the hell can I find

Chorus
The real love if it ain't here
If this is it why the fear
Of an induced prison in the house
Lost in confines of this brain

Escape, escape you fool of fools
Trying to find eternal love—you're not cool
Your rest is what you hold in hand not heart
And it's a lovely place to be…

Written May, 1980

Like The Mystery

Like the mystery of the deep blue sea
Baby we can be—something together
In all kinds of time, all kinds of weather
We'll make it through—together

It's like a dream the verse above
We are divorced but still share a love
I had a mistress, my addiction to Mr. Jack
You're happily married again, I'm alone and that's a lack

Did we forget our vows on the grass at Emory
Twenty years of marriage I still have a good memory
I'll never forget my mixture of coffee and Jack
It was a shock to you and I will tell you that

Now I'm widowed from my last wife
It was OK but there was some strife
A stepfather to two and I said oh no
I'm a friend not a father—was I stuck for life

Now I've calmed down—quit Mr. Jack
Quit smokin' two packs—they kill you two packs
Three glasses of wine just once a week
I love my dreamy memories—not for the meek

Written Feb.2, 2005

To Travel

Sometimes it's better to travel and arrive
Does your creek contain water that was snow a
    while ago
After hitching cross the country you wander in tired
Saying sometimes it's better to travel than arrive

Through the dark aspens and bright grass and mountain
    shrubs
You see the country we left behind affectionately
Your eyes have played tag with peaks above
The wind moans of my love

Your spirit kept you going up and down the trail
Was it love or just some kind of sign
I believe the former not the latter in kind
So love me baby satisfy my mind

Have you found an exit from the cave around you
Are the stalactites in your eyes
I've found the door and here it is
It is all within your head

A Piece of a Bottle

A piece of a bottle
Is all that I have
To see me though another day
Alone in this house

My friends are all busy
Got fun things to do
But me and my bottle
Got fun things to do too

Chorus
We might have us an adventure
All over this house
It'll be like the old days
People jumpin' all about
But when this bottle is empty
It'll come back to me
'Bout how me and this bottle
Replaced you and me

Might pick up my guitar
Might write us a song
'Bout me and this bottle
And being all alone

Written by Tam Duffill & Sand Reid 8-14-77

Angel Wings

Oh yes I can talk, yes I can sing
of my sweet lovely Angel Wing
She sent me the book I read every night
right or wrong—yes I know I am right

She helped save me, oh yes it's true
Without your hugs and prayers, yes I am blue
I wear your pin just above my heart
You may think I'm not—but I could be smart

Oh yes with Faith and all the Grace I need
I am hungry oh yes I will feed
Oh had some bad times—put me down
Tried to run a straight line—but I go 'round

'Round to your love I need it so bad
If I ain't got it I feel so sad
Where are you my sweet Angel Wing
I have to shout—I have to sing

Sing of your love—I want it for me
The world may say I don't—but yes I see
Of your love it is written in red
Oh Angel Wing help me fly to heaven after I'm dead

Chorus
Angel Wings shine your light on me
Oh sweet Angel shine loving light on me
I'm not afraid with Angel and the Lord on my side
Angel Wings shine your light on me

TWD, August 2006

Talks To Jesus

I need a woman, yes I do
To get away from these lonesome blues
Like oh Sweet Angel way back in my history
If I only knew then—but now I see

Chorus
Are you a prophet or disciple or man who talks to Jesus
I just know I do it and it could be because
I have been close to death many times
Got closer to God and my faith is mine

Oh my Angel with blond hair and blue eyes
I'd steal you if I could but theft is not my game
So I wish you well and know God is the same
One that I have and that is tame

Sometimes it's never long enough when I say my prayers
But I send my love to you and you know I care
Care for my faith in you—take it to your grave
To be buried in the heavenly yard and you know
     you're saved

TWD, July 2007

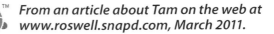 *From an article about Tam on the web at www.roswell.snapd.com, March 2011.*

Rockabilly Hall of Fame legend and Recording Artist Tam Duffill was recently discovered at Dogwood Forest in Marietta. Tam (Tamson Wailes Duffill) was born in November 1940 and was originally from Bremerton, Washington. At age 16 he and his family moved to Fairhope, Alabama. Tam's basic start in music began when he heard Jimmy Rogers. When Tam was twelve years old, he bought his first guitar. His natural gift to play, sing and write music led him at age 16 to write and then record his first record for RCA "Cooly Dooly" (Groove label) in 1962; the reverse side of the record was "You Put The Hurt On Me." (Photographs by Tom Blanton)

DUFFILL

Tam Duffill I've seen him longhaired shorthaired bearded cleanshaven straighthealed freakedout up and down, seen him swingin his legs off a porch railin on Monroe naked to the waist takin the sun, seen him head back foot banging tamborine mouth wideopen singing in the Bistro and the Barrel and the Station, singing *John Brown*, I remember him singing *John Brown*.

Tam Duffill married January five years back still a student in Alabama College. Montevallo; out of Washington State a baby into Arlington Virginia where the grateful dead of the nation sleep like John Brown into Alabama's Mobile;

Tam Duffill strong and well-put-together make his father the admiral proud; shy and talking poetry please his mother. In the house use his right hand like the people, outside throw a ball with his left like himself. (The right lobe of the forebrain controls the left side of the body, and vice versa, keep that in mind.)

Tam Duffill teaching history in Savannah and Jonesboro high schools, singing, teaching, singing again; young teacher, good teacher according to the students. No doubt disturbing to the older staider steadier more singleminded faculty.

Tam Duffill never singleminded, throwing with his left hand, eating with his right: weak and strong, beautiful and ugly like the rest of us, married, father and divorced in three years' time.

Tam on mescaline and grass, grass every day, up every day until he became seer and prophet and poet, messagebringer who could not speak the words of his message, prophet whose messages stuck in his throat: singer and teacher without song or lessons; singing and wishing he were teaching, teaching and wishing he could sing.

Tam with more words than he could speak more lessons than he could learn grabbing back into the past with if onlys toward happier more ignorant yesterdays, relying back and farther back (far enough back is a time when you were not) until Joyce, *exwife* and dear friend, and other friends, could help him no more.

Tam in Grady and Georgia Mental Health, scoffing up a bottle of sleeping pills and getting pumped out, floating and prophesying on a grass cloud on weekends; varityping sometimes trying to build a bridge of work and words back somewhere, helping Joyce one weekend talking guns, leaving with one of his two pistols, leaving the rifle;

Tam Duffill saying Joyce, whatever, don't hold yourself responsible:

Tam with a bullet in his head (shot in the right temple which controls the left side, across the frontal lobes it fetched up against the skull on the left side which controls the right half of the body; shot right through the speech centers which had worked so hard and so well and still would not sing what he had to sing nor teach what he had to teach: a shot which fetched up on the left against the skull, the skull which had to be carved to allow for the swelling on Monday night and on Wednesday night they were saying if can live for 48 hours then he'll pull through but what that bullet's carved out no man can tell) no man will tell: the beautiful dumb wise sad son of a bitch may have lost the very part that was hurtin him most: *if your right eye offends you*

Tam, Tam, twominded Tam: shot by himself or another, who knows, but anyhow wanting bad not to be or not to be now or not to be him now, with a bullet track all across the inside of the front of his fine head, staggering and walking and stumbling like a deer shot on the neck for a hundred and fifty feet for the help nobody had been able to give him for twenty-eight years.

—og

From the archives of *The Great Speckled Bird*, (Vol. 1, No. 25, 12/09/1968). This article was written by the late Irving (Bud) Foote under the name "Og King of Bashan."

Tam Is Still With Us

You can believe in life after death or not, but since his passing, Tam seems to still be around. I say this because so many synchronicities have occurred, and continue to occur, as Donna Overall and I have tried to complete this book.

To refresh your memory, a *synchronicity* is an occurrence that is so out the ordinary that it cannot be thought to happen just by chance. It is a word that was coined by Carl Jung. The first such occurrence happened at the funeral.

I had been keeping the book *Stride Toward Freedom* by Martin Luther King, Jr., at my home for Tam because he was afraid it might be stolen at the assisted living home. The book was valuable because it was signed by Dr. King. I had it with me at the funeral to give to Brian. As I was showing the book to people, I found a note in the book from Tam to me that had been there for years. All this time I had the book, I had never discovered that note.

The second synchronicity happened just a few weeks after the funeral. I was looking through an index box of recipes, and I found another note from Tam. Again, it was a note that had been there for many years. I had no idea that it was there, and no memory of putting it there. It was an old handwritten Valentine's Day note from Tam to me.

Tam had given me his car, a 2001 Toyota Corolla, just a few weeks before he died. I had been driving it, and the door handle on the driver's side opened without any problem. A few months after he passed, I went out to get in the car, put the key in the lock, and the door would not open. My first thought was, Tam does not want me to sell his car. Chris and I had four vehicles at the time, which was very impractical for two people. I was reluctant to sell Tam's car right away, for two reasons. I was sentimentally attached to it, and it had a handicap sticker. At the time, I had plantar fasciitis, and it was hard for me to walk very far.

I knew I would have to sell his car at some point, and I was thinking about doing it soon because I had an interested buyer. When the door wouldn't open, I was sure it was Tam's way of letting me know he didn't want me to sell it. I called someone I trust who can channel. She told me Tam was saying that he wanted me to keep the car and use the handicap sticker until my foot was well. He was saying that I had always taken care of him and this was his chance to take care of me. She said that he was never very far away and that I should talk to him whenever I felt I needed to. She said if I tried to unlock the car door the next morning it probably would work. The next morning when I tried, it *did* work.

I told a few close friends this story—the ones that wouldn't think I was crazy. This convinced me more than ever that Tam really was still around.

Months later, as I was working on this book, several times I needed to go back to the original to look at something I had typed to see if I had made an error. I would go right to the exact page of the original without having to thumb through the pages. This happened over and over as if Tam was guiding me to the correct page. It felt like this was precisely what Tam was doing. I found myself exclaiming aloud, "Tam, are you standing behind me looking over my shoulder?"

Donna Overall had the same experience when she was working on the book alone, as well as when we were working together. We were at the computer making corrections, and although we were ready to upload the book and publish it, apparently Tam did not agree. Donna was unable to upload the file in spite of several attempts. She has been through this process many times with no trouble, but Tam knew there were still some corrections that needed to be made. We looked through the book again and found several more errors that we had missed.

We were both convinced Tam was taking a big interest in his book and wanted it to be correct. After I left, Donna tried to upload the file again and failed. Once again, Tam wasn't satisfied, and he seemed to help Donna find the mistakes we had missed easily.

I called my trusted friend with the gift of channeling, and I was reading to her from Tam's book. She stopped me and said, "He's coming through." This was a few months ago, and I can't remember everything he said, but I'll tell you as much as I can. He said he was with a group of others and that they were there to help me. That I had been asking for help. This is true. In my daily prayers I say, "Help me grow spiritually, dear Lord." He said that I was the only one that had ever truly seen and understood him as his deepest Self. He said that I still felt guilty for leaving him and that I should not. We had a contract before we came back to earth together, and when we completed the work we needed to do together, it was time for me to leave. Everything happened as it was supposed to have happened. I should let go of any guilt that I have. I did everything I was supposed to do.

Then he said, "Do you have any questions?" This caught me off guard. I didn't know what to ask. It seemed like a once in a lifetime chance, and I felt unprepared. I asked, "Is there anything else that I am supposed to do?" He said, "You have done more than enough. Look for me in the clouds, the trees, and flowers and you will see my smile. I am never far away."

Tam is still very much with us. You can believe or not. I choose to believe.

—Marianne Duffill Cox

Made in the USA
Charleston, SC
26 July 2015